THE COMIC-STRIPPED AMERICAN

WALKER AND COMPANY
NEW YORK

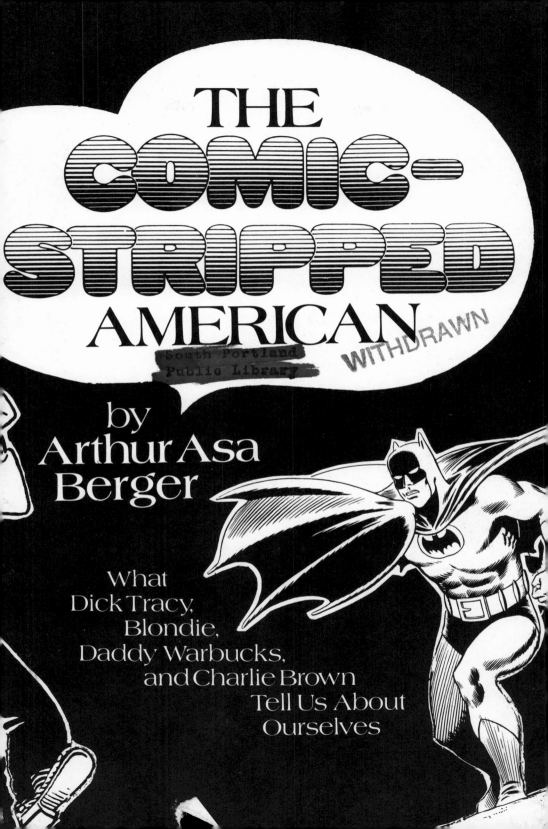

THE COMIC-STRIPPED AMERICAN

WITHDRAWN

by
Arthur Asa
Berger

What
Dick Tracy,
Blondie,
Daddy Warbucks,
and Charlie Brown
Tell Us About
Ourselves

The author gratefully acknowledges permission to reprint the following articles:

"Dagwood in the American Psyche," *Human Behavior*, January 1973. Copyright © 1972 *Human Behavior* Magazine. Reprinted by permission.

"Eroticomics" *Social Policy* Sept-Oct. 1970. Copyright Social Policy Corporation, New York.

First published in the United States of America in 1973 by the Walker Publishing Company, Inc.

Published simultaneously in Canada by Fitzhenry & Whiteside, Limited, Toronto.

ISBN: 0-8027-0430-1
Library of Congress Catalog Card Number: 73-83299
Printed in the United States of America
Designed by The Etheredges

10 9 8 7 6 5 4 3 2 1

to Ida Krebs

CONTENTS

PART III. THE AGE OF CONFUSION:
THE THIRD GENERATION OF COMICS

ACKNOWLEDGMENTS

I have greatly benefited from the ideas and works (and, in some cases, the friendship) of the following people:

Sigmund Freud, Bronislaw Malinowski, Marshall McLuhan, Martin Grotjahn, Mulford Q. Sibley, Alan Dundes, David Noble, Max Goldberg, Robert Tucker, Giuseppe Gadda Conti, Richard Hoggart, Roland Barthes, Umberto Eco, Edgar Morin, Gerald Grow, Sigfried Giedion, Harry Geduld, Ray Browne, Marshall Fishwick, David Manning White, William E. Porter, Stan Lee, Ralph Ross, S.I. Hayakawa, Agostino Lombardo, Russel Nye, John Cawelti, Erik H. Erikson, Al Capp, John Heher, Jim Arnquist,

S. Gorley Putt, Stanley Milgram, Franco Ferrarotti, Charles Schultz, Dick Demorest, Charles Winick, Leo Lowenthal, Warren Bennis, Geoffrey Gorer, Margaret Mead, Johan Huizinga, Edward T. Hall, Tom Wolfe, Fustel de Coulanges, Carl G. Jung, Brom Weber, Benjamin DeMott, Mircea Eliade, Orrin E. Klapp, Erving Goffman, Harold Garfinkel and Ernest Dichter.

I am grateful to all the comic strip and comic book artists (and their syndicates) who have allowed me to use their work. And last, but not least, let me express my sincere appreciation to Dedria Bryfonski, my editor, for her kind and helpful assistance with this book.

The great artist necessarily has his roots very deep in his own time—roots which embrace the most vulgar and commonplace fantasies and aspirations.

MARSHALL McLUHAN, *The Mechanical Bride.*

FOREWORD

It is difficult to judge the quality of a comic strip in the manner that one would judge a painting because a comic strip does not stand as a single work of creation. Even though each daily feature has to be entertaining and attractive in itself, the quality of a comic strip is judged by whatever it is that has made it last over a period of twenty or thirty years.

Inevitably, it is the lead character that we think of when we discuss a successful comic feature. We rarely recall any particular episode, but we recall instead the visual characteristics and unique personality traits that the character has had. Developing such a character and surrounding him or her with a supporting cast and then sustaining them over a period of time requires a unique sort of energy. It is this, I think, that separates the good comic strips from the ordinary ones. Newspapers have a way of coming out every day, thus forcing the cartoonist to keep an extremely demanding schedule; seven ideas a week, every week of every year.

If the cartoonist possesses any sort of artistic or competitive drive, he wants these ideas to get better all the time. Thus he is forced into a race with others in his field, and it is not one where there is any time for coasting. The strips have to be drawn regardless of what is happening in the cartoonist's personal life. I have the feeling that there have not been too many comic strip artists who have been successful at doing this, but being very close to the problems perhaps hampers me from being a good judge.

It is interesting that Arthur Berger has his own kind of energy to make him want to examine these various comic strips and try to come to conclusions of his own. I am pleased with what he has done in this book, and I am convinced that it performs a service which all of us in our profession appreciate.

CHARLES M. SCHULTZ

INTRODUCTION

Since this is the first book that I know of which deals with the way comics reflect our culture, I feel that I owe my readers an explanation of how I came to write this book, and why I wrote it. Although comic strips and books have long been part of the American imagination, they have received almost no serious attention. (My earlier book, *Li'l Abner: A Study in American Satire,* is one of the few exceptions.)

I like to think of myself, then, as a pioneer. There have been many articles and books on the history of the comics, but they have all been quite general, if not superficial. Critics of literature and sociologists have done some preliminary explorations around the fringes of the bush, but I am the first academician to plunge into the jungle, to investigate this virgin land of the American imagination with any thoroughness.

There are several reasons why comics have been ignored. It may be, as many would argue, that there is little of significance in them, and that it is a waste of time to take them seriously. Proponents of the "comic books as junk" position argue that they are mechanical, sub-literary items manufactured to please the lowest common denominator, and not worth bothering with. There is so much to be done with Henry James, Faulkner, and other of our greatest writers that they claim we haven't got the time to spend on "inferior" forms of culture. Thus graduate students go through our significant and less significant American writers and thinkers with fine-toothed combs, while the "junk" that hundreds of millions of people read is almost totally ignored.

There is an elitist bias to most of our academic work. We are so intoxicated with the greatest that has been thought and said that we forget about the common man. We also assume that the culture of the common man is insignificant and deny ourselves a perspective on life that might act as some kind of corrective to the distortions we get by limiting ourselves to a view from on high.

I'm not arguing against studying high culture; I'm just suggesting that there are other dimensions to our culture, other perspectives, and that they deserve the same kind of investigation. As a matter of fact, much of our high culture is influenced by our popular culture. Marshall McLuhan points out that Joyce was steeped in "lowbrow" culture and used it in writing *Ulysses*.

I would also claim that popular culture, mass culture, whatever you wish to call it, has—in certain cases—literary, artistic, and philosophical significance, in its own right. And I will try to demonstrate, in this study of our comics, that there is a great deal of culturally interesting material to be gleaned from them.

ARTHUR ASA BERGER

THE COMICS PAGE, VALUES,
AND AMERICAN SOCIETY

All of a sudden America has discovered popular culture. It has always been there—but because it has been so ubiquitous and all-pervasive we never really noticed it. Perhaps our current concern with violence has led us to wonder if there is some connection between the mass media and everyday life. Whatever the case, we have lately become conscious of our general environment and there has been an explosion of interest in it—both in its physical manifestations (ecology) and its cultural ones (particularly popular culture).

Most of our attention (literally and figuratively) has been directed toward television, the dominant medium of our time, whose impact upon our psyches and the social fabric has yet to be fully understood. But not very far behind television in terms of popularity is the comic strip, a form of mass culture that has been around for many decades as an important ingredient of our daily newspapers.*

Although comic strips do not have the psychological impact of television, numerous studies have demonstrated that comics do play an important role in the lives of the people who read them—as sources of diversion, escapism, and information about life.† It is obvious, of course, that the terms "comic strip" or "funnies" are no longer appropriate. A large number of them have not humor but crime, adventure, or love as their basic, theme. And the talent in the creators of these strips ranges from the comic genius of George Herriman (*Krazy Kat*) to the brilliant satiric inventiveness of Al Capp (*Li'l Abner*) and the morbid grotesquerie of Chester Gould (*Dick Tracy*).

Relevance is everything to contemporary mass culture criticism. For something to be popular, it must deal with themes that are meaningful to large numbers of people. That is why conventions in the various popular art forms are important. If we accept the hypothesis that our popular arts mirror our culture, that somehow they are tied to our

---

* See E.J. Robinson and D.M. White, "Who Reads the Funnies—and Why?" in D.M. White and R.H. Abel, *The Funnies: An American Idiom*, Free Press, 1963. They argue that comics are more popular (in terms of exposure) than any other medium.

† See the following: *The Sunday Comics, A Socio-Psychological Study of Their Functions and Character*, Social Research, Inc. 1955 and Arthur Asa Berger, *Lil Abner: A Study in American Satire*, Twayne Publishers, 1970.

concerns and based upon widespread assumptions, then the study of our popular culture becomes an important means of understanding our society. To the extent that some of our comic strips appeal to the mythical lowest common denominator, so much the better for social scientists who want to know something about the mythical common man who is a big part of this "lowest common denominator."

Acting upon the assumption that the comic strips which have appeared in our newspapers have some significance for our society and are a social record of sorts, I made a pilot study of the comic page in *The San Francisco Chronicle* from 1926 to the present. I selected the years 1929, 1938, 1947, 1956, 1970, and 1973 for my analysis, since that configuration provided an evenly spaced distribution for this pilot study.

My research involved the following topics:

1. Incidence of violence in the strip. I defined violence as the direct use of physical force against another or any expression of hostility involving the use of a weapon or the intentional causing of hurt, even in humorous strips.

2. The number of strips per page.

3. The number of words per page.

4. The proportion of men and women.

In addition, I selected at random a page of comics for an "impressionistic" sociocultural analysis, to show how the comic page lends itself to investigation.

TABLE I: VIOLENCE IN THE DAILY COMICS PAGE

Date	Total Number of Incidents	Incidents of Humorous Violence
January, 1929	3	0
January, 1938	3	1
January, 1947	11	1
January, 1956	11	0
January, 1970	0	0
January, 1973	6	5

These figures suggest that violence is quite a negligible aspect of the daily newspaper comics. If there are an average of three or four frames per strip and eight strips per page, we find that there will be something like five hundred frames in any given month (and this is a low estimate). When, out of a possible five hundred frames you have a dozen incidents of violence, some of which are humorous in nature, it is obvious that violence is a relatively unimportant part of the daily comic page. This is not true of adventure and humor comic books, in which a high percentage of the frames involve physical combat and violence.

One reason there is so little violence now is that few of the strips are in the action-adventure category. The number of strips in this category has declined to two as of 1973: *Dick Tracy* and *Steve Roper. The San Francisco Chronicle* is probably unusual in this respect. Recent concern with violence may be another factor.

TABLE II: WORDS PER PAGE, MALE AND FEMALE
FIGURES PER PAGE*

Date		Strips	No of Words†	Average words per strip	Male-female Ratio	
January 7,	1929	5	740	148.0	21	12
January 10,	1938	11	900	81.8	54	24
January 7,	1947	9	675	75.0	41	20
January 12,	1956	8	440	55.0	48	6
January 14,	1970	8	365	45.6	22	15
January 13,	1973	8	410	51.0	31	5

* All human male and female figures were counted (even if the same figure appeared in several frames) each time they appeared. These figures represent the number of male and female appearances, not the ratio of individual males to females. The dates were randomly selected.

† To nearest five.

Several things are apparent from this analysis. First, the number of strips has remained fairly constant—around nine for more than twenty years. *The San Francisco Chronicle* carries other strips elsewhere in the paper, but the comic strip page has been fairly regular in the number of strips carried.

Second, the number of words per page (and strips) has decreased markedly. A glance at the earlier strips verifies this. Thirty years ago a strip would carry hundreds of words, with the script taking perhaps half the space in a given frame. Now, with the development of closeups and non-continuity strips, and perhaps owing to the competition from television, comics offer much less in the way of dialogue. Thus the page in 1929 with only five strips has more than twice as many words as the eight-strip 1973 page. The strips carried by *The Chronicle* are noted in Table III.

Third, male-female ratios show an almost two-to-one male dominance. Furthermore, women in the comics tend to be characterized as love objects, one more complication in some male's pursuit of power and glory. The comics, as well as other forms of popular art, make use of sex as a complication and an attention getter. On the visual level, there is much in the way of girlie art in the comics. The first strip in *The Chronicle* (1970) is about a model, Tiffany Jones, who is often shown dressing and undressing, and upon occasion has bared her delicious breasts to the viewers. There is a good deal of low-keyed eroticism in the comics—and in some cases, not usually found in daily comics, or on the comics page, flamboyant eroticism, and even pornography —although the definition of that term is one that seems to resist resolution.

TABLE III: STRIPS ON COMIC PAGE OF THE
SAN FRANCISCO CHRONICLE

Year	1929	1938	1947
Strips on Page	Gumps	Mutt & Jeff	Terry & Pirates
	Gasoline Alley	Tailspin Tommy	Dick Tracy
	Moon Mullins	The Gumps	Gasoline Alley
	The Bungles	Gasoline Alley	Moon Mullins
	Ella Cinders	Moon Mullins	The Gumps
		Dixie Dugan	Gordo

Year	1929	1938	1947
	Oliver's Adventures (started Jan. 20)	Dick Tracy Pop Smitty Mickey Finn The Bungles	Dixie Dugan Joe Palooka Smilin Jack
Total	6	11	9

Year	1956	1970	1973
Strips on Page	Dick Tracy Joe Palooka Terry & Pirates Jackson Twins Gasoline Alley Gordo Dr. Guy Bennett* Ferd'nand	Tiffany Jones Dick Tracy Apartment 3-G Steve Roper Odd Bodkins Gordo Fred Bassett Miss Peach	Steve Roper Apartment 3-G Dick Tracy Gordo Miss Peach Fred Basset Doonesbury Broom-Hilda
Total	8	8	8

* as of Jan, 9th Steve Roper instead of Dr. Bennett

It can be seen that the morality rate for comics is quite high. Only *Dick Tracy* and *Gordo* have lasted since 1947. *Odd Bodkins* was dropped from the *Chronicle* and reinstated a short while later (due to pressure from fans) which meant that *Robin Malone*, a dreary strip, was canceled. *Odd Bodkins* was then dropped for good, a short while later, to make room for *Doonesbury*, one of the new wave comics.

Having looked at violence, the amount of dialogue and male-female ratios from an historical perspective, the question of how the comic strip can be more fully exploited by the social and cultural historian suggests itself. Anthropologists do a great deal with myths and archeologists with fragments of pots. What can we do with comics—other than wrap garbage?

One answer to this question has been provided by Francis E. Barcus, whose study of Sunday comics offers us a very comprehensive methodology for analyzing comics based on considerations such as the subject of the strip, the goals of the characters, and the means used to achieve these goals. The conclusion he reaches in this study is important for us:

> There is a consistency in the mass media view of life. Dramatic and fictional materials in the form of magazine fiction, and the comic strip all present basically the same view. There is also a consistency over a period of time. *Although the comic strips, perhaps more than other media, relate to the current scene—indeed, draw much of their material from it*—the staple commodities, the quick identification of characters through easy stereotypes, do not change rapidly. [My emphasis]. *

If, as he suggests, the comic strip relates "to the current scene," then it certainly demands serious study, which, to this point, it has seldom received. I have provided, in a somewhat compressed format, the categories used by

* Francis E. Barcus, "The World of Sunday Comics," in D.M. White and R.H. Abel, *The Funnies: An American Idiom*, Free Press, 1963.

Barcus in his study of the Sunday comics, which can be adapted by investigators wishing to study comics.

TABLE IV: ASPECTS OF THE COMIC STRIP (AFTER BARCUS)

Aspect of Life Category

Domestic Relations	The Supernatural
Crime	The Entertainment World
Nature and Animals	Race and Nationality
Armed Forces and War	Education and Schools
Love and Romance	Science and Scientists
Business and Industry	Literature and Fine Arts
Government and Public Affairs	Religion
Historical Events	Age of Characters
Male/Female Ratio and Relations	Citizenship, National Origin
Social Class	Marital Status

Type of Comic Strip

Humor	Fantasy
Real life	Serious

Major Goals of Characters

Safety, self-preservation, escape from consequences of crime
Health, physical and mental integrity
Individualism, self-expression
Financial security, wealth, material success
Pleasure, self-indulgence, thrill, adventure, impulse
Power, mastery over others
Love, friendship, affection, companionship
Prestige, fame, honor, recognition, respect, popularity
Justice, duty, public service, "doing right," law and order
Reform, altruism, idealism for better life or world
Progress, creation, invention, knowledge, search for truth
Hatred, revenge, spite, fury, defiance
Escape from routine of everyday life

Means to Achieve Goals

Personal	*Impersonal*
Violence	Established authority
Deceit	Luck, fate, chance
Personal charm	Other (misc.)
Industry	
Dependence on others	

* Research for this section was supported by an institutional grant to San Francisco State College by the National Science Foundation.

Keeping these various (and multifarious) aspects of comic strips in mind, let us take a look at a page of comics to see how we can interpret this social record. I have selected the comics page for January 22, 1970, because it contains many aspects of current history which are still in everyone's mind. Comic strips must always be studied in conjunction with history. I might also caution that the comic strip is an *iterative* art form, so that the events of a given day in a given strip have meaning in terms of past events in the strip. Comic strips carry their history with them, we might say, and we must keep this in mind. (This problem is best overcome by doing a long-term study of a strip or the strips on the page.)

While this particular day's comics might seem, on first glance, to have little in the way of social relevance, there are a number of interesting considerations:

1. The landscapes in both *Dick Tracy* and *Apartment 3-G* reflect the modern urban setting, and a segment in *Odd*

Bodkins deals explicitly with the problem of smog.

2. *Apartment 3-G* deals with the world of corporate high finance and certain American Dream virtues such as individualism and hard work as a source of security.

3. The authoritarian father in *Fred Basset* is outwitted by the dog, who in obeying the spirit but not the letter of the law triumphs.

4. *Miss Peach*, though about toddlers, deals with the pecuniary nature of many relationships between men and women. It also touches briefly on the whole matter of consumerism.

5. The art work is, for the most part, quite crude. Except for *Tiffany Jones*, an English fashion strip, and *Apartment 3-G*, none of the strips is drawn very well.

6. The page divides itself into two segments—the top half being serious and involving adventure, romance, crime, and the bottom half involving humor—with animals, children, odd creatures, etc.

Even this rather casual analysis of one day's comics shows that they have a considerable social dimension—both in terms of the topics discussed and certain attitudes revealed.

I have attempted, in this study, to offer some hard facts about the newspaper comic strip and to encourage others to give more serious attention to this neglected art form which has a good deal of information about the social record. For any medium that has the continued attention of hundreds of millions of people deserves serious attention and study.

PART I

THE INNOCENTS

THE FIRST GENERATION OF COMICS

The comics I have classified as innocents are those which appeared from the turn of the century until approximately 1920. These strips had a certain naive vitality to them which was an accurate reflection of the age. This period was, according to Henry May, "The Age of American Innocence" (to adapt the title of his well-known book). He describes the ending of American innocence as follows:

> The war and its emotions passed with extraordinary suddenness. To see the full meaning of the story that ended in 1917 it is necessary to look beyond the wartime enthusiasm and beyond the complementary savage disillusion of the post-

war years. At some time long after the Armistice whistles had stopped blowing, it became apparent that a profound change had taken place in American civilization, a change that affected all the contenders in the prewar cultural strife. This was the end of American innocence. Innocence, the absence of guilt and doubt and the complexity that goes with them, had been the common characteristic of the older culture and its custodians, of most of the progressives, most of the relativists and social scientists, and of the young leaders of the prewar Rebellion. This innocence had often been rather precariously maintained.

Certainly there were exceptions to this view of the world, but as a rule, innocence is an excellent way of characterizing the climate of opinion of the era.

The more important comic strips originating in the age of innocence reflect this innocence in a graphic way. They are:

The Yellow Kid	1895
The Katzenjammer Kids	1898
Happy Hooligan	1899
Foxy Grandpa	1900
Buster Brown	1902
Little Nemo	1906
Maude the Mule	1906
Alphonse and Gaston	1906
Mutt and Jeff	1907
Bringing Up Father	1913
Krazy Kat	1913
Boob McNutt	1918

The cut-off date for first-generation innocent comics is

approximately 1920, when the second generation of modern and serious comics begin.

The first-generation strips tended to be humorous, though as I have pointed out, some serious themes can be found. The very titles of the strips suggest the kind of innocent lightheartedness and playfulness that characterized these strips. We have come to recognize that humor is a very complex matter, and beneath what seems to be comic absurdity and mindlessness are often profound psychological forces. I have tried to deal with some of these hidden elements, pointing out unconscious as well as conscious motivation, covert as well as overt meaning.

The art work in these strips tends to be simple and crude—perhaps as unrealistic as the ideas people supposedly had about the world in the age of innocence. In this respect, the innocence of the childlike drawings, and the often infantile nature of the strips all fitted together perfectly. We had to wait until our post-innocent, post-childlike era for our comic strips to lose their comic, humorous nature and be drawn in a realistic style. There were exceptions to the simple, cartoony style—Winsor McCay's *Little Nemo* was beautifully drawn and almost surrealistic in terms of the quality of its fantasy—but for the most part, the strips were crudely drawn.

In examining the first generation of comics (and, for that matter, all of the comics) I have found a number of important themes and values that help explain, I believe, their psychocultural importance. I assume that these comics strike some kind of a chord in their readers' imaginations and aid them in working out their own psychological problems. I also assume that they reflect cultural values and that a serious analysis of comics is a contribution to American social history.

THE YELLOW KID
Urban Poverty in the Good Old Days

The Yellow Kid, generally credited as the first American comic strip, is intimately tied up with the development of newspaper technology. According to Stephen Becker (in *Comic Art in America*), the foreman in Pulitzer's color press room needed the chance to print a solid block of yellow, found a drawing by Outcault that suited his purposes, and *The Yellow Kid* was born. Had the color, yellow, not been a difficult one to print at that time, *The Yellow Kid* might have been a different color, and yellow journalism— named after *The Yellow Kid*—would probably be tied to a different hue.

Colton Waugh (in his book *The Comics*) described the

Yellow Kid in the following picturesque manner:

> . . . a strange creature who, though evidently a boy, ap-
> peared to have passed through the major experiences of life
> in the first six months. Though small, he was important-look-
> ing. His head, bald, with flap ears, had a wise, faintly Chi-
> nese face, and he looked directly into the reader's eyes with a
> quizzical, interrogative smile, half timid, half brash, as if he
> understood perfectly well the portentous event which was
> happening through him.

The first appearance of *The Yellow Kid* was on July 7, 1895. The Yellow Kid became extremely popular, evoking, according to Becker, "that first, gentle wave of mass hysteria which accompanies the birth of popular art forms. The Yellow Kid was soon on buttons, cracker tins, cigarette packs and ladies' fans; eventually he was a character in a Broadway play."

This ability of comic strip characters to capture the public fancy, and to be exploited for commercial gain, still remains strong. In recent years there have been *Shmoo* crazes, *Batman* crazes, and we are in the middle of a long, drawn-out *Peanuts* craze, in which Schultz's characters seem to pervade every aspect of American life.

Thus the pattern set by *The Yellow Kid,* which was an instrument in a circulation-building effort, has continued to this day. Comic strip figures can be commercially exploited in many ways and in many media—there have, for example, been Broadway plays about *Li'l Abner, Superman,* and *Peanuts,* and all have been successful.

Outcault's drawings are exceedingly busy, sometimes

with as many as fifty human figures and a half-dozen (or more) animals of various kinds. All of this is in addition to numerous signs, posters, and exclamations made by the characters, and an urban scenario with detailed drawings of buildings and trees. You have to spend a good deal of time reading all the signs and piecing things together. There is no development and sequential pattern; rather, there are tableaus that have to be scrutinized and digested in a leisurely manner, owing to their complexity—though on occasion Outcault had episodes with a number of panels. It might even be asserted that *The Yellow Kid* represents a basic thrust in the direction of the comic strip as we know it, with episodes, gags, and characters which have an historical dimension.

Hogan's Alley, the locus of The Yellow Kid and his pals, is a squalid slum, inhabited, it turns out, by brutalized and grotesque characters. Most of the characters are children, though these children (like the characters in *Peanuts*) are not childish. Many wear derbies, some smoke cigars and cigarettes, and others are bearded. They are ragamuffins, children of the poor, and, as such, are allowed all manner of exotic actions. In a graphic manner they represent the mysterious world of the poor, a world also made famous by Horatio Alger, except that Alger's heroes were able to struggle upward and escape from poverty. Outcault's grotesque children seem to revel in it. To all outward appearances, they have rejected the American Dream and are content with their lot. Either that, or they are incapable of escaping from Hogan's Alley and the degrading environment in which they live.

One of the basic myths in America is that the poor are happy with their lot, and that they have certain satisfactions which middle-class and upper-class people do not have. The poor fascinate the other classes, who find them both an object of interest and of scorn. According to the myth, people are poor because they do not wish to be otherwise; they have repudiated the Puritan ethic and must pay for it. This gives us a justification for our scorn. Thus by making romantic figures of the poor, we relieve ourselves of the obligation to aid them.

But there is more to the ugliness and squalor of Hogan's Alley and the grotesques inhabiting it. The characters may be fascinating and contemptible, but their very existence is problematic. And Outcault's remarkable draftsmanship served to *focus attention on the problem of poverty*, even if he had ulterior purposes for using his poverty-stricken characters. There is a great deal of ugliness in the strip. The main character, The Yellow Kid, looks (but does not act) like a cretin who has escaped from an asylum; and many of the other characters are often shown with looks of anguish and terror on their faces.

The faces of the inhabitants of Hogan's Alley reflect the grim despair which gripped the country in the last few years of the nineteenth century. The Pullman Strike had occurred in 1894, and the country was racked by a depression. Ignatius Donnelly had warned, in a speech in 1892, that America was in a state of crisis and at "the verge of moral, political and material ruin." He said:

The urban workmen are denied the right of organization for

self protection; imported pauperized labor beats down their wages; a hireling army, unrecognized by our laws, is established to shoot them down, and they are rapidly degenerating into European conditions. The fruits of the toil of millions are boldly stolen to build up colossal fortunes for a few, unprecedented in the history of mankind, and the possessors of these in turn despise the Republic and endanger liberty. From the same prolific womb of governmental injustice we breed the two great classes—tramps and millionaires.

Hogan's Alley and its inhabitants, then, represented everything that was anathema to the American democrat. Thomas Jefferson had warned the nation to avoid industrialization and urbanization, but we had not listened.

And so people became piled upon one another, as he predicted, and the natural rural American, "nature's nobleman," was rudely shoved out of the picture to be displaced by hordes of European immigrants—whose spawn peopled Hogan's Alley. The Yellow Kid's world was that of tough, dirty little immigrant kids and disheveled old women with sad eyes and a hopeless look on their faces. There were Negro children, with kinky hair or thick white lips, Irish toughs, and mangy, ragged animals. The ambience was chaos, with bodies sticking up everywhere and crowding the space in the cartoon, just as it was felt that we were beginning to get crowded in America.

In *The Yellow Kid,* the sense of fantasy and use of humor masked a sense of despair. In one cartoon, "The Children's Beauty Contest in Hogan's Alley," children are hung out on a line, like clothes, and others are tied to hooks. Babies and children permeate the cartoon and you

WHAT THEY DID TO THE DOG-CATCHER IN HOGAN'S ALLE

The Yellow Kid

get a sense that they are not really human; they are "material" to be manipulated. Outcault (and his successor Luks) have a number of gags and crazy things going on, but you cannot help feeling a kind of repugnance about all the squalor and confusion.

There was a good deal of reference to politics in *The Yellow Kid*. One episode was devoted to the gold-and-silver question, which figured large in the McKinley-Bryan election of 1896. The Yellow Kid's robe says " 'fer O'Brien. At last I am inter politics." And there were a number of other signs and posters referring to gold and silver.

As a result of the very complicated machinations of Outcault, who switched from Pulitzer to Hearst and back, and then elsewhere, George Luks ended up drawing *The Yellow Kid,* and Outcault did a different strip, *Buster Brown.* Luks's work is, at times, even more complicated than Outcault's, with even more screaming children and barking dogs and riffraff, but the essential formula, that of the tableau with signs and puns and jokes, was not changed. Eventually the public lost interest in *The Yellow Kid* as sequential gag strips such as *The Katzenjammer Kids, Happy Hooligan,* and *Foxy Grandpa* appeared on the scene. *The Yellow Kid* was static and quite crude, as were most of the early strips. (Though merely a decade removed from *Krazy Kat* in time, *The Yellow Kid* was very far removed from it in style.)

The humor of *The Yellow Kid* was most revealing. I will talk about the grotesque later (in *Dick Tracy*), which can be seen as a visual manifestation of social pathology. In theory, a society which creates grotesques must, in some way, be grotesque itself. What must be understood about the grotesque is that it is profoundly intellectual, in essence. As David Worcester says in *The Art of Satire:*

> By making us accept an eccentric, or grotesque, scale of values in opposition to our normal scale, the author creates positive and negative poles. Across the gap leaps the spark of irony. The secret of detail in grotesque satire is that its ultimate appeal is to ideas.

The same can be said of the use of the grotesque in comics and other forms of graphic media. The norms are repudiated and there is a suggestion that something is askew.

The language in *The Yellow Kid* makes use of a number of comic techniques. There is misspelling, which is a way of revealing ignorance and is part of the humor of exposure and embarrassment. We gain a sense of superiority when the ignorance of others is revealed. We also find a good deal of word play in the strip. Outcault and Luks were both quite facile, and delighted in manipulating (as well as manhandling) language. They abandoned the rules of spelling and used "de" for "the" and "dese" for "these," in an attempt to capture the idiom of their earthy guttersnipes.

But the humor only masks realities. Underneath the horseplay and absurdity we find a world of anguish and pain. *The Yellow Kid* is not really an innocent entertainment. It has social dimensions even though they are not apparent. It expresses, though perhaps not consciously, a sense of malaise, a feeling that the old, rural, natural America is being destroyed. The spatiality of the tableaus is interesting; everything is crowded and chaotic, and there is a certain nihilistic exuberance in the strip that is at once comic and menacing. One reason for *The Yellow Kid's* great popularity must have been that Americans saw themselves in it, even if reflected in a distorted manner. It offered some laughs to a society in the midst of turbulent struggles and great anxiety. It made comic allusions to politics and society, and reflected rather closely the quality of life at the turn of the century for the average working man.

At this time the average worker in America earned between four hundred and five hundred dollars a year, which is equivalent to fifteen hundred dollars a year by today's standards. The period has been described as follows in Dye and Ziegler, *The Irony of Democracy*:

> Unemployment was frequent, and there were no unemployment benefits. A working day of ten hours, six days a week, was taken for granted. Accidents among industrial employees were numerous and lightly regarded by employers. The presence of women and children in industry tended to hold down wages but was an absolute necessity for many families. . . . Child labor was ruthlessly exploited in the cotton mills of the South, in the sweat shops of the East, and in the packing plants of the West.

Small wonder, then, that the faces of the inhabitants of Hogan's Alley reflect a worldliness and bitterness that we do not now associate with childhood. In those days, children (and all the poor) were fodder for an industrial behemoth that ground them up in its quest for profits and which loudly proclaimed, as its credo, "The public be damned."

(These words were spoken by William H. Vanderbilt of the New York Central Railroad.)

Perhaps that is what we find in Hogan's Alley—the damned, who have almost abandoned hope and are trying to salvage a bit of pleasure from their desperate situation. It might even be asserted that there is a certain amount of heroism in these kids; they still have spirit and energy, a spark of social awareness, and a sense of humor, despite it all.

The Yellow Kid has generally been looked upon as a humorous strip. But just as humor is often a mask for aggression, so is the comic nihilism of *The Yellow Kid* a rather transparent cover which allows a glimpse into the despair and degradation of millions of Americans. It stands as a testimonial to the inadequacies of our society in the mauve decade.

The kids in *The Yellow Kid* are abandoned—left to their own devices by parents presumably too busy, or too tired, to look after them. This theme, that of the "abandoned" child, is a recurrent one in the comics. We find many heroes and heroines in the comics who are abandoned for one reason or another. Superman, Batman and Little Orphan Annie are orphans; Robin is Batman's ward; the characters in *The Yellow Kid* are left out in the alley to play. This sense of having *been* abandoned is intimately related, I believe, to the American historical experience of *abandoning* the old world, our "fatherland," and coming to a new world where there were opportunities for improvement. There is a heavy psychological price to be paid for casting out on one's own—and the idea that one can and should do this is with us today; it may be that many run-aways, hippies, and sleeping-bag wanderers are dropping out on their own before they will be (so they feel) abandoned by their parents, who have different values and different life styles, but who still act on the principle of abandonment.

Outcault started a strip called *Li'l Mose* in 1897, and it turned into *Buster Brown* in 1902. Buster Brown lived in a different world from that of The Yellow Kid. The setting was one of middle-class affluence—good manners, a kind bulldog named Tige, and domestic comedy. *Buster Brown* was a great success; like *The Yellow Kid, Buster Brown* was commercially exploited, and to this day there is a company manufacturing Buster Brown shoes. But the move into domestic comedy took the bite out of Outcault's style, and *Buster Brown,* is, for the most part, a rather simple and innocuous strip. It is quite likely that Outcault and his public did not appreciate the social significance of *The Yellow Kid,* that they did not recognize the memorable evocation of social pathology behind the zany tricks of the inhabitants of Hogan's Alley.

THE KATZENJAMMER KIDS
Infantile Disorders of the Left
and Right and Center

The Yellow Kid was not really a comic strip. It was a tableau with a great deal of language and action, but it was not sequential. The format of the comic strip, as we know it today, came with Rudolph Dirks's *Katzenjammer Kids*, which first appeared on December 12, 1897. In this strip we find the essential ingredients of the comic strip as listed by Pierre Couperie and Maurice C. Horn (*A History of the Comic Strip*): ". . . narrative by sequence of pictures, continuing characters from one sequence to the next, and the inclusion of dialogue within the picture."

Dirks was influenced a great deal by the work of Wilhelm Busch, whose *Max and Moritz* is the prototype of *The*

Katzenjammer Kids. Couperie and Horn's description of the strip is quite revealing:

> Situated at first in an undefined country, then in an imaginary East Africa land (perhaps the former German East Africa colony), if not in Polynesia, this strip related in a frenzied style the war to the death carried on by two rascals, Hans and Fritz (the Katzenjammer Kids, more affectionately nicknamed the "Katzies"), against any form of authority, whether parental, educational, or governmental. The mother of the two urchins (die Mama), their adoptive father (der Captain, a former shipwrecked sailor rescued by die Mama), der Inspector (representing the school authorities), are all the butt of a systematic campaign of sabotage that successfully resists spankings, threats, and promises.
>
> Dirks did not use dialogue in the early strips, but very soon his characters were speaking an Anglo-German pidgin, the effect of which was as devastating as the incredible diabolical tricks of Hans and Fritz. "The Katzenjammer Kids" is not a simple strip of comic adventures, but a genuine tale of destruction incarnate, in the twin person of Hans and Fritz, for whom, in the Inspector's apt words, "society iss nix."

This passage captures the general flavor of the strip and some of its more important themes, but Couperie and Horn neglect a most significant factor—the inevitable punishment the twins must undergo for their misdeeds. Generally, Hans and Fritz are punished in the end, both literally and figuratively. Thus the Puritan notion that one must pay for one's sins is present in the strip, lurking beneath the chaos and confusion. At times, when the twins are sinned against by adults, it is the Captain and his cohorts who are whacked about by Mama. But the notion that you can't get away with anything, no matter how ingeniously you try, is an essential element of the strip.

In an early strip, on January 16, 1898, we see an example of this. Hans and Fritz, having seen a man carrying home a rocking horse, tie boards on a live goat, much to the goat's annoyance. In the course of trying to ride him, however, both kids are knocked to the ground and inadvertently thrashed by the goat, who wanders off awkwardly at the end of the tale, leaving the two ragged, bedraggled kids behind him.

The Kids, compulsive practical jokers, are never discouraged, however. They never learn. Year after year they continue with their tricks, and year after year they pay for it—usually by getting a strenuous thrashing. The conflict between the Kids and the Captain, and other adults in the strip, can be attributed to the generation gap. In the perspective of the comics it is an old theme, and its existence at the turn of the century suggests that generational conflict is a basic and long-time constituent of the American social personality.

Naughty boys play a special role in American culture. Talcott Parsons has explained this phenomenon (in "Certain Primary Sources and Patterns of Aggression in the Western World"). His analysis seems remarkably appropriate to the dynamics of *The Katzenjammer Kids:*

> In addition to the mother's being the object of love and identification, she is to the young boy the principal agent of socially significant discipline. . . . When he revolts against

identification with his mother in the name of masculinity, it is not surprising that a boy unconsciously identifies "goodness" with femininity and that being a "bad boy" becomes a positive goal.

The mother is the central figure in the moral universe of the bad boy, and this is reflected in the strip. Mama, with her ever-ready rolling pin—a symbol of pleasure (pies) as well as pain—is ready to clobber the Captain and the Inspector, and anyone else who violates the rules and does naughty things like swiping pies. Since goodness is allied with femininity, boys are forced to be naughty to prove their masculinity, and the parent is then pushed into a highly ambivalent situation. If the little boy is obedient, the parent fears he will not turn out to be a man, so, in a sense, he is proud of the naughty little boy. Yet the tricks the naughty boy plays are a source of embarrassment to the parent, who must somehow figure out a way of preventing the "bad boy" from going too far.

Further, children, who seem to perceive everything, recognize that beneath the feigned embarrassment of the parent is a certain kind of pride and relief; thus the child is motivated to continue with his disruptive behavior. In *The Katzenjammer Kids* an important central theme is food. Everyone is very oral, and Mama's pies and other culinary creations generally occupy the center of attention. At this level it is all quite innocent; in the strip the naughty boys confine their attention to food and similarly minor matters. So do the Captain and his friends. There is a vague sexual aspect to the basic punishment of the Kids, for getting spanked is slightly erotic. But the strip tends to avoid anything overtly sexual; it seems to have stopped at the oral stage. The cross-eyed mother is not an appealing figure from a sexual point of view; but she can sure cook! Everyone in the strip tends to be pop-eyed and cross-eyed. Dirks (and Knerr, who did a rival strip when legal difficulties led to Dirks's abandoning *The Katzenjammer Kids* for a similar strip—*The Captain and the Kids*) drew his figures in a highly stylized manner. The characters generally have large eyes, bulbous noses, and short, squat, dumpling-like bodies. The figures are quite wooden, though Dirks was able to give their faces a great deal of expressiveness.

The blacks in the strip fitted into the stereotype of the time—the African savage with a fancy little loin dress and names like "Captain Oozy-Woopis" or "King Doo-Dab." In an adventure dealing with pranks at school, one little boy is called "Sammy Snowball." The Kids get their friends all dirty, when they start playing around with ink, but Sammy, because he is already black, is not punished by the irate teacher. As he leaves, he says, "Ise glad ise black." In this episode there is a little "goody-goody" named Percival de Puyster, who represents the "poor (effeminate) little rich kid." He comes to school with a new white sailor suit and the Kids play leapfrog over him with ink-stained hands, thus ruining his suit.

Actually, blacks were not really objects of ridicule in the strips. They were drawn according to the cartoon convention of the time (which still exists to this day, in many

cases), but in the stories they didn't play the "Sambo" role, and possessed a certain amount of dignity and authority, given the ethos of the strip.

The question arises concerning who is responsible for the Kids's lack of development. After all, one of the functions of parents is to help children become civilized, to help them grow up and gain a measure of self-control. But the Kids refuse to do this; they remain eternally infantile, with *no control over their impulses*—and, in fact, influence the Captain, the Inspector, and other adults. The Kids have been arrested in their development, we might say; the only blood relation in the strip, their mother, controls them (and everyone else) by punishment, but she does not help the Kids grow up.

Thus, we find manifestations of generational conflict and anarchistic, impulsive behavior in one of our earliest comic strips. The Kids are the dominant figures, with the mother, and then the Captain and his friends, all playing supportive roles. This breakdown in terms of power relationships exists to this day, as a matter of fact. It is a function of our equalitarian ethos. Seymour Martin Lipset quotes from a number of visitors to the United States in the nineteenth century and concludes in *First New Nation.*

If these reports from the middle and late nineteenth century are reminiscent of contemporary views, it is still more amazing to find, in a systematic summary of English travelers' opinion *in the last part of the eighteenth and early years of the nineteenth centuries,* that the emphasis on equality and democracy had *already* created the distinctive child-oriented family which astonished the later visitors:

"A close connection was made by the stranger between the republican form of government and the unlimited liberty which was allowed the younger generation. . . . They were rarely punished at home, and strict discipline was not tolerated in the schools. . . . It was feared that respect for elders or for any other form of authority would soon be eliminated from American life. . . . As he could not be punished in school, he learned to regard his teacher as an inferior and disregard all law and order."

Aside from the slapstick spankings of the Kids, this passage seems to describe the situation in the strip quite well. The Kids do not accept any authority as valid; they never internalize any notions of respect for others or appropriate behavior in social situations. They are punished for their actions, but they do not concede their point—namely, that no authority is valid.

Thus they remain free to play their next prank. The spanking is included in the calculus of pleasure and pain by which they operate. It does not serve as a deterrent, but is merely written off as an overhead expense. The psychoanalytic aspects of "kidding" have been explored by Martin Grotjahn in *Beyond Laughter* and are most relevant:

The term "to kid" means to treat somebody like a child— "kid" being an almost universal vernacular for a little child. Like teasing, kidding contains an element of cruelty. The kidder uses his advantage of superior experience, knowledge, or authority to assume a pseudo-authoritarian, powerful, and hostile attitude toward the victim. The threat is pretended, not realized.

The inveterate kidder expresses his own conflict with authority (usually with his parents) and projects it onto his victim.

Kidding, Grotjahn explains, is intimately related to playing practical jokes, which are enactments of the verbal aggression found in kidding. It is the aggression which is significant here.

The Katzenjammer Kids is really an extended series of
practical jokes, usually "played" on adults by the Kids
(though occasionally the reverse is true). The problem of
aggression is never solved: the pattern is aggression, followed by punishment, followed by aggression, and punishment, *ad infinitum.* Of course, much of this serves the
requirements of the comic gag strip and the fact that humor
is intimately related to masked aggression. But in the case
of *The Katzenjammer Kids,* the aggression is extremely evident and perhaps even dominating. The strip is really a
slapstick bag of tricks, and as is the case with slapstick, the
aggression is not only overt but is often messy and crude.

Though the humor is simple and often vulgar, the strip
provides a valuable record of some of the social and psychological forces operating upon the American psyche at
the turn of the century. Our earliest real comic strip shows
that anti-authoritarianism has long been a part of the American character and that the child-centered family tyran-
nized over by impulsive little brats is not a recent phenomenon. The generation gap is reflected here along with the
dominating sense of retribution for sins. The latter is problematical since the belief in the inevitability of punishment
does not deter the Kids from their pranks: it is actually
part of the psychology of Puritanism. The belief in predesti-

nation actually spurred people on to great efforts during Puritan times, just as the Kids's knowledge that they would almost surely be caught and punished inspired them to pull off bigger and more absurd pranks.

The continued popularity of this strip leads me to suspect that the problems it points up are still with us. Quite likely, most readers do not recognize the significance of the strip, so far as various unconscious anxieties and difficulties are concerned. Yet I believe that it does somehow speak to people and that they recognize important matters are being dealt with, underlying the slapstick humor and anarchistic madcaps.

The rather devious history of the strip—or actually of the two strips—suggests that *The Katzenjammer Kids* has played a rather important role in American popular culture, and in the American imagination. When Dirks left the *New York Journal,* he lost rights to the name of the strip, *The Katzenjammer Kids,* but he was given the rights to the characters. Thus, in 1913, there were two versions of the same comic strip: one drawn by Dirks, and the other drawn by Harold Knerr, who were both inspired humorists. When the World War I broke out, *The Katzenjammer Kids* was transmogrified into, of all things, *The Shenanigan Kids,* and everyone became Irish, in spite of their pidgin German dialect. After the war, when anti-German feelings cooled down, the strip was given its original name again, and it continues in publication to this day, one of our great comic strip classics.

MUTT AND JEFF
The Politics of Failure

Mutt and Jeff, which first appeared on November 15, 1907, and is still going strong, has the distinction of being the first *daily* comic strip. It has been appearing, more or less continually, for some sixty-five years—a phenomenal example of the ability of the comic strip to resist the pressures of time and decay. Only *The Katzenjammer Kids,* which started a decade earlier, is more long-lived. In both cases (and generally such is the case with successful comics), the strip continued on after the death of the original artist. Thus certain characters take on a semblance of immortality and attain a dimension that might be described as mythic.

Mutt is a lean, tall, would-be operator. He is a compul-

47

sive gambler who spends a great deal of his time looking for a stake and a great deal of his money on the wrong horse. All of his scheming and manipulating are for naught, for he is always unlucky. He refuses to bow to his fate, however, and continues on—hoping for a lucky break. This is actually an important part of the American character—the notion that failure is no reason for abandoning hope. There is always another chance, and a success after many failures tends to validate the past and justify past failures.

Mutt is a comic figure—the shrewd operator who continually bungles things—of a stock American type. He is best described as a *comic rogue,* a kind of fool described in Orrin E. Klapp's *Heroes, Villains and Fools* as a kind of prankster, or rascal:

> . . . who goes so far in mayhem that he almost joins forces with the villain. He is found in comic strip characters like Dennis the Menace, Krazy Kat, the Katzenjammer Kids, Little Kayo, Wimpy and Happy Hooligan. Lying, stealing and brick-heaving are his stock in trade. He approaches the flouter and deceiver among villains. Just as the antic fool suspends decorum, the rogue suspends *morality* in an unreal world of farce and outrageous situations (the clown burglars talking loudly as they climb through a window, the adulterer caught under a bed) that in real life might result in a riot or a call for an ambulance.
>
> Such noncomforming types . . . provide a vacation from conformity but nevertheless affirm the order they seem to flout, though in different ways (deformed and strange fools by holding up negative models, antic fools and rogues by catharsis through vicarious misbehavior and the spirit of carnival).

In Mutt's case, the fact that he generally does not suc-cessfully carry off his schemes, or is duped by Jeff, rein-forces the social order even more directly. It is all pretty harmless and silly stuff, and we always know what will hap-pen, yet we can't help admiring Mutt's determination to triumph over the malevolent fates which conspire to thwart him. He is a clown or a fool but has a resilience and an imagination of almost heroic proportions.

Locked in a struggle for dominance with Mutt is his runty little friend Jeff, nicknamed for Jeffries. Jeff's name and top hat suggest something of the aristocrat. Moreover he is also a fool, and first met Mutt in an insane asylum. Jeff is a symbol representing the basic equalitarianism in the American psyche. Top-hatted upper-class types are fools, just like people from the lower classes. And making him a little person adds to the leveling effect.

The battle between Mutt and Jeff has been seen as that between the "big guy" and the "little guy," and in such cases the average American roots for the underdog. But Jeff's relation to Mutt is a complicated one, since Mutt is his benefactor, in a sense. This is explained by Gilbert Seldes in *The Seven Lively Arts:*

> The historic meeting with Little Jeff, a sacred moment in our cultural development, occurred during the days before one of Jim Jeffries' fights. It was as Mr. Mutt passed the asylum walls that a strange creature confided to the air the notable remark that he himself was Jeffries. Mutt rescued the little gentleman and named him Jeff. In gratitude Jeff daily sub-mits to indignities which might otherwise seem intolerable.

In all fairness to Mutt, however, I should point out that he has generally been driven to violence by Jeff's bungling.

This is part of the genius of the strip: A confidence man is inexorably linked up with a nincompoop who compromises or ruins everything. In later strips Jeff becomes more autonomous and comes off much better; but in the early days he frustrates Mutt's plans regularly, and gets a brick on the head, or a whack for his pains. This has been going on for sixty-five years, but Mutt still tempts the fates. This kind of repetition is actually tied to our sense of logic and the iterative nature of comics. The repetition can involve action or language, but in both cases the humor stems from the structure of the situation and the suspense created by the series.

In *The Anatomy of Criticism,* Northrop Frye explains the function of repetition in our humor:

> The principle of humor is the principle that unincremental repetition, the literary imitation of ritual bondage, is funny. . . . Repetition overdone or not going anywhere belongs to comedy, for laughter is partly a reflex, and like other reflexes, it can be conditioned by a simple repeated pattern.

> The principle of repetition as the basis of humor both in Jonson's sense and in ours is well-known to the creator of comic strips, in which a character is established as a parasite or glutton (often confined to one dish), or a shrew, and who begins to be funny after the point has been made every day for several months.

Thus Mutt and Jeff have a historical dimension, and those who have followed their activities for a number of years understand (in some way) the significance of a given day's adventures. After we have known Mutt and Jeff for a number of years they become part of us, so to speak, and each day's installment becomes part of a biography. It is part of their biography, our biography, and the nation's history.

Mutt and Jeff is one of those rare social artifacts that spans profound changes in a nation's historical development. Some Negroes alive in 1907, when the strip first appeared, had been slaves. Men were alive then who had fought in the Civil War; and the children who read it were to fight in world wars, in Korea and in Viet Nam. The Gold Strike had been made but a few years before, and the West was not very far removed from primitiveness. The year *Mutt and Jeff* appeared was the year Henry Adams published *The Education of Henry Adams*. Mark Twain, Howells, and Henry James were still alive. It was a time that, from present-day perspectives, seems lost in the dim past, an America that bore little resemblance to the modern super-society we live in. *Mutt and Jeff* spans progressivism, the New Deal, and the Great Society, as well as the great crash and the depression; it spans the horse and buggy and the moon probe.

Through all of this wander two men who are to suffer endless reversals and indignities (Mutt later is to marry and become involved in domestic intrigues). They reflect, in a vague way, a sense of the futility of it all, which leads me to suspect that *Mutt and Jeff* questions the myth of the self-made man. Desire and will power may be necessary, but they are not sufficient and do not guarantee success. On close reflection, *Mutt and Jeff* is really about failure.

This theme is cloaked in absurdity and slapstick comedy, but failure is an essential aspect of the strip. Mutt's name is significant; it is an abbreviation for muttonhead, a stupid person. He is stupid for thinking he can pick winning horses or make his schemes work out. He is also stupid for relying on Jeff, a boob.

In truth, the strip is not very far removed from the theater of the absurd, which shows similar kinds of figures and relationships. Both *Mutt and Jeff* and the theater of the absurd have in common a diffuse kind of pessimism which permeates all the inane comedy. It may very well be that the strip expresses a profound sense of doom, revealed by all the abuse which both of the characters suffer.

There is a good deal of violence in the strip—usually in the last panel, when Jeff is conked with a brick or punched in the head, the power of the blow illustrated by the inevitable "Pow!" But violence in *Mutt and Jeff,* and in many strips, is a convention that has a special meaning to the readers of comic strips. When Mutt throws a brick at Jeff, or socks him, the violence is a kind of playful or comic violence which has no lasting effect, though Jeff may get a black eye or a big lump on his head. These lumps are his rewards for infuriating poor Mutt, and they are as much an expression of love as of anger. Expressing anger is something which most Americans are taught to avoid—with dire consequences, since the resentment inevitably is manifested in various unhealthy ways. (See this topic in my discussion of aggressive passivity in *Blondie.*)

This violence is actually part of the humor of action, and involves the matter of "degradation." Slapstick violence is a kind of degradation which generally has the effect of reducing the victim to the status of a child who can be punished legitimately for his naughty ways. He is deprived of any sense of dignity; his adult status is shown to be a fraud. In reality, we are told, he is an infant.

Continual exposure to this form of harmless violence may also be a factor in the average American's matter-of-factness about violence. A good cause, we learn in *Mutt and Jeff,* legitimizes violence, and the brick thrown by Mutt is not far removed from the massive violence sanctioned by Americans in Viet Nam, for instance, where we believed we could force our enemies to the peace table. They were to play Jeffs to our Mutt, in our mind's eye, except that never having been socialized by the comics they didn't acquiesce, and things didn't turn out as we wished.

Part of the violence in the strip is a reflection of the violence permeating American society. We have a heritage of frontier lawlessness, intensified by our equalitarian value system. Because we do not admit anyone's superiority we ultimately are forced to take matters into our own hands, since nobody has enough status to force us (morally speaking) to accept arbitration. In a society that emphasizes the individual, it is only natural to expect Americans to insist upon personal, immediate, direct, and often violent solutions to difficulties.

Thus Mutt often relieves himself of his aggressive and hostile feelings by whacking Jeff; in this respect violence is as American as apple pie. Though the violence in *Mutt and Jeff* is comic violence, and a conventional comic strip resolution of frustration (and a way of ending a strip), it is, nev-

ertheless, violence, and as I pointed out earlier, constant exposure to violence may well desensitize a person to it. Indeed, we continually find comic violence permeating the humorous comic strips—as well as the serious violence in the adventure strips. The Katzenjammer Kids are continually spanked, Popeye punches people around, and even Lucy, in *Peanuts,* thrashes people from time to time.

It is ironic that a country with so much concern for the rights of the individual and for self-sufficiency was raised on a diet of comics which showed people continually being degraded and humiliated. Violence is related to the term *violate,* which suggests that violence somehow assaults the autonomy and dignity of a human being. In truth, individualism in American history was generally a meaningless euphemism to beguile large numbers of people who were being subjected to the violence of inhuman and dangerous jobs for paltry wages. In this respect the comic violence in *Mutt and Jeff* was a somewhat distorted reflection of the brutalization and exploitation suffered by the ordinary man in the course of his work and life. The humor in *Mutt and Jeff* tends to be simple, coarse, and rather inane—though the strip is often funny. Perhaps it has been popular for so long because its readers look at it and see themselves, though I believe American society has changed considerably since the strip began and has become much more humanized.

I have been focusing upon the psychological significance of the violence and various other themes which I note in the strip. When Mutt hangs Jeff on a meathook, after some zany episode, it is an example of slapstick buffoonery

which people tend to laugh at and dismiss without considering the implications of the act. It may well be that I
have overemphasized the violence and depersonalization
(hanging Jeff on a hook next to chickens makes him less
human and more of a chicken, after all), but I have done
this because, so often, people tend to neglect everything but
the narrative elements in a comic strip.

Mutt and Jeff is a classic strip, appreciated by James
Joyce and others with avant-garde sensibilities, as well as
by the common man in America. But it is also a mirror in
which some of our social and psychological problems and
aberrations are humorously reflected.

KRAZY KAT
The Social Dimensions of Fantasy

Krazy Kat is the most admired of American comic strips and is generally conceded to be the most imaginative and remarkable example of the comic strip art form ever to have appeared. Gilbert Seldes, the dean of popular culture critics, wrote about it in ecstatic terms in *The Seven Lively Arts*:

> *Krazy Kat*, the daily comic strip of George Herriman is, to me, the most amusing and fantastic and satisfactory work of art produced in America today. With those who hold that a comic strip cannot be a work of art I shall not traffic. The qualities of *Krazy Kat* are irony and fantasy. . . . Mr. Herriman, working in a despised medium, without an atom of pretentiousness, is day after day producing something essen-

tially fine. It is the result of a naive sensibility rather like that of the *douanier* Rousseau; it does not lack intelligence, because it is a thought-out, a constructed piece of work. In the second order of the world's art it is superbly first rate—and a delight.

This passage comes from a celebrated essay, "The Krazy Kat that Walks by Himself." In it Seldes explores the significant aspects of the strip—its lyricism, surrealism, and the bizarre relationship that exists between its main figures, Krazy Kat, Offissa Pupp and Ignatz Mouse.

His description of the plot is excellent:

. . . Krazy (androgynous, but according to his creator willing to be either) is in love with Ignatz Mouse; Ignatz, who is married, but vagrant, despises Kat, and his one joy in life is to "Krease that Kat's bean with a brick" from the brickyard of Kolin Kelly. The fatuous Kat . . . takes the brick, by a logic and a cosmic memory presently to be explained, as a symbol of love; he cannot, therefore, appreciate the efforts of Offisa B. Pupp to guard him and to entrammel the activities of Ignatz Mouse (or better, Mice). A deadly war is waged between Ignatz and Offisa Pupp—the latter is himself romantically in love with Krazy; and one often sees pictures in which Krazy and Ignatz conspire together to outwit the officer, both wanting the same thing, but with motives all at cross purposes. This is the major plot; it is clear that the brick has little to do with the violent endings of other strips, for it is surcharged with emotions. It frequently comes not at the end, but at the beginning of an action; sometimes it does not arrive.

The basic plot of Ignatz throwing a brick at Krazy (who

takes the brick-throwing as an act of love due to "racial" memories), and Offissa B. Pupp, intervening and sometimes jailing Ignatz, is subject to countless variations. The relationship, curiously enough, is similar to that found in Sartre's *No Exit,* in which a male character loves a lesbian, who loves a female character, who loves the male character. It is an impossible situation that leads to the conclusion that "hell is other people." The relationships are impossible, so that the play is at once comic, or perhaps "absurd" would be better, and tragic.

In *Krazy Kat* the relationships are further complicated by the fact that animals who are natural enemies are hopelessly in love with one another. Thus Offissa B. Pupp, a dog, loves Krazy, a cat, who in turn loves Ignatz, a mouse. Furthermore, Ignatz, instead of being a meek, mild little creature, is shown to be an antisocial, anarchistic, monomaniacal figure who has no fear of either cats or dogs. If Ignatz is not really like a mouse, Krazy is not typical of cats. Krazy is not independent, haughty, or aloof the way cats tend to be. Cats are often disagreeable, passive, and hostile—and if television commercials are truthful, exceedingly fussy eaters.

Krazy is just the opposite. He is loaded with personality, wit, and love—especially with love for an animal which cats usually hunt and eat. All of this gives the strip a fantastic quality which is furthered by Herriman's remarkable landscapes and incredible prose. The strip was so unique, and so obviously the product of a singular sensibility, that when Herriman died in 1944, it was not continued. The fantasy in *Krazy Kat,* said Robert Warshaw, "sometimes becomes mechanical, but it is never heavy and it frequently achieves the fresh quality of pure play, freed from the necessity to be dignified or 'significant' and not obviously concerned even with entertaining its audience" (*The Immediate Experience*).

Warshaw mentions some attempts to read meaning into *Krazy Kat,* but is not sympathetic with them:

> Offissa Pup is the sole authority in the universe and Ignatz the sole evildoer. Evil always triumphs—Ignatz always throws the brick; but authority always triumphs, too—Ignatz is always put in jail. Krazy lives happily between the two. It is a very nice universe for Krazy; if there is an issue, Krazy does not understand it; he loves to be hit by the brick, but he respects Offissa Pup's motives.

> One is tempted to read into this the meanings that one finds in the serious world of respectable culture. E.E. Cummings talks in his introduction about the opposition between the individual and society. But if Ignatz and Krazy are very good examples of individuals, Offissa Pup is not much of a society: his jail is always empty the next day. *We do best, I think, to leave "Krazy Kat" alone. Good fantasy never has an easy and explicit relation to the real world.* [My italics.]

I do not agree with Warshaw at all. He is not really correct about what goes on in the strip, and his assertion that *Krazy Kat* should be left alone, and not explicated, strikes me as naive. It may not be *easy* to understand fantasy and show its relation to the world, but that is no reason for not trying. Warshaw's notion seems inherently romantic; we are, I assume, to have some kind of a sublime relation to

the strip—but not to analyze it, as if to do so would some-how destroy the magic. I would argue that really under-standing it will increase our appreciation of it, as a work of art and as something that does have social significance, even if this social dimension is not easy to see.

Some comic strips, such as *Li'l Abner, Little Orphan Annie,* and *Dick Tracy,* are quite obviously loaded with social and political references and are much easier to in-terpret than *Krazy Kat.* They have caricatures of promi-nent people, make allusions to social and political phenom-ena and, on occasion, comment explicitly on politics. *Krazy Kat* does not do this, but nevertheless it reflects, in varying ways, American values and character and has a social di-mension. This is because, so social psychologists tell us, in-dividual acts are not just the result of impulses and atti-tudes dominating the minds of individuals but are also "the product of the external circumstances of their life, such as their economic, political and religious institutions, or [the] general state of their society." (Z. Barbu, "Social Psycholo-gy" in N. MacKenzie, *A Guide to the Social Sciences.*)

If such be the case, the attitudes found in the various characters, the kinds of heroes they represent, the personal-ity configurations, the kinds of humor and themes all have a social dimension, even though *Krazy Kat,* as a fantasy, seems very far removed from the world of politics and from society *per se.*

Let us take an example of some significance—Krazy's attitude about the brick that Ignatz continually heaves at him. Krazy has an elaborate rationalization to explain why the bricks thrown at him are not symbols of aggression and malevolence. Seldes describes the situation:

> It is the destiny of Ignatz never to know what his brick means
> to Krazy. He does not enter into the racial memories of the
> Kat which go back to the days of Cleopatra, of the Bubastes,
> when Kats were held sacred. Then, on a beautiful day, a
> mouse fell in love with Krazy, the beautiful daughter of Kleo-
> patra Kat; bashful, advised by a soothsayer to write his love,
> he carved a declaration on a brick and, tossing the "missive,"
> was accepted, although he had nearly killed the Kat. "When
> the Egyptian day is done, it has become the Romeonian cus-
> tom to crease his lady's bean with a brick laden with tender
> sentiments . . . through the tide of dusty years" . . . the
> tradition continues. But only Krazy knows this. So at the end
> it is the incurable romanticist, the victim of acute Bo-
> varyisme, who triumphs; for Krazy faints daily in full posses-
> sion of his illusion, and Ignatz, stupidly hurling his brick,
> thinking to injure, fosters the illusion and keeps Krazy
> "heppy."

The point is that Krazy refuses to face the fact, so to speak,
of Ignatz's ill will, and reinterprets it so as to transform it
into an expression of love. *This tendency to value illusion
over fact seems to me to be an essential aspect of American
character.* We call ourselves realists and pragmatists, but
(at least until recently) we subscribe to the American
Dream, and think of ourselves as innocents and American
Adams, each in complete control of his destiny.

In this respect there is a strong similarity between
Krazy and his illusions and the average American who believes in the American Dream and in the myth of the self-
made man. In both cases belief overwhelms reality, though,

in all fairness, there was (historically speaking) some reason for believing that you could rise on the social ladder in the frontier society of the nineteenth century. Statistics show that social mobility in contemporary America and Europe are not very different, and such has been the case for a number of years.

It may also be that Krazy's "racial" memory is as faulty as our historical one. The legendary nineteenth-century American *individualists,* pioneers and inner-directed men of popular imagination have now been shown to be "other-directed conformists," which means that one more illusion has been shot down. De Tocqueville talked about the mass man in *Democracy in America,* and if Seymour Martin Lipset is correct, there have been no fundamental changes in American character from the nineteenth to the twentieth century. Filled with illusions about his past and his future, it has been hard for the typical American to face reality, which is one reason the United States is a most backward industrialized nation in terms of social welfare programs.

Of course *Krazy Kat* is not the real world, and in that fantasy world illusion supports both Krazy, who interprets the bricks as signs of love, and Ignatz, who derives great pleasure from "creasing" Krazy whenever possible. Love will conquer all, Krazy believes—incurable and indomitable romanticist.

If fortitude and endurance in the face of what seem to be hopeless odds is one theme of *Krazy Kat,* another important one is rebellion and submission. It is this theme which led E.E. Cummings to talk about the relationship between the individual and society, as represented by Ignatz Mouse and Offisa B. Pupp. The idea of a willful, egotistical, antisocial, anarchistic *mouse* is brilliant. Ignatz, in a sense, refuses to acknowledge his mousehood (being a good American mouse he opts for illusion) and becomes, instead, a brick-throwing menace, always testing authority and generally paying the consequences—confinement in jail. Many of the strips end with Ignatz peering out from behind bars in jail. But while he has submitted to power and authority, in the form of Pupp, he has not changed. We know that the next day, God willing, he will heave another brick.*

Ignatz's willfulness is directly related to the American egalitarian *ethos* and to our faith in will power. In a society where everyone supposedly has equal opportunities, the only significant differentiating factor becomes will. Ignatz is willful, but he does not use his will constructively—which demonstrates that there can be negative aspects to will power. It can be abused. Ignatz is a monomaniac who has channeled his will very narrowly and is constrained, one might say, to be the menace he is. It might even be that he has a longing for jail, for some kind of control over his anarchistic and self-destructive impulses.

Will power, along with belief in nature and providence, were the three concepts central to the nineteenth-century mind, according to John William Ward, in *Jackson: Symbol for an Age*. These notions were read into Jackson's life by the people of the time, who created him in their own image, so to speak. They also recognized the danger of un-

---

* Recent evidence suggests that Herriman was a Negro posing as a white, which would explain the two significant themes—illusion and rebellion-submission.

harnassed will power, and so sentimentalized Jackson and had him submitting to higher authority, lest his will become a dangerous instrument. We have always feared power in America, whether it be will power or political power, and have never been at ease until we felt that there were some constraints on power.

It is this sensibility, manifested in such things as the American rooting for the underdog, and believing in equality of opportunity, which requires that Ignatz be sent to jail. This prevents him from changing from mouse to behemoth or leviathan, and reassures us that power will not get out of hand. I do not think that Herriman had any thoughts such as I've outlined above, but being an American with American values, his attitudes toward will and power took the form they did. In my analysis of attitudes toward authority in American and Italian comics I discovered that American animals reflected our anti-authoritarian values (and often triumphed over human beings), while just the reverse was so in Italy, where authoritarian values are dominant.*

One of the most striking things about the characters in this strip is their measure of authenticity. Given the ambience of the strip—absurdity, with changing landscapes, mad logic, and fantastic rhetoric—the characters manifest a remarkable degree of courage and transcendent love. They are very much like the existential heroes of contemporary literature, who find life absurd, but maintain, in the face of this absurdity, courage and commitment. Ignatz is an autonomouse character and Krazy, obviously believing that existence precedes essence, refused to be placed in cat-

* See "Authority in the Comics," *Transaction*, December, 1966.

egories which deprive him of his dimensionality.

Krazy and his friends were existential heroes before *we* discovered existentialism. In the face of inevitability (such as Sisyphus faced) they maintain humor, courage, and dignity. In an absurd world that is always changing from one moment to the next, they are committed and purposive, even if we consider their commitments rather odd. Frederick R. Karl and Leo Hamalian's discussion of the existential hero (in the introduction to *The Existential Imagination*) explains this matter better:

> If the individual accepts Kierkegaard's challenge and seeks his religious center within himself, then he begins his fierce encounter with nothingness. Man here floats in a foreign world in which human existence is feeble, contradictory, and contingent upon an infinity of other forces. Nothing can be certain except the individual's certainty of his own response. All he can hope to know is that he is superior to any universal or collective force, and to recognize that the universal or collective force can never understand the individual. He must be alone; for in his very aloneness is his salvation.

Gilbert Seldes sensed this quality in the strip, which is why he called his essay "The Krazy Kat that Walks by Himself." Krazy and all his friends represent an affirmation of the human spirit that has universal appeal, though its emphasis on will has particular roots in American beliefs about the self-reliant individual. In this case self-reliance extends beyond the confines of man's relation with society; it "takes on" the very universe, and has cosmic (as well as comic) significance.

PART II

THE MODERN AGE COMICS

THE SECOND GENERATION—
OR, AFTER THE FALL!

The second generation of comic strips are those which appeared from approximately 1920 to 1960. During this period many of our most famous and most familiar strips made their appearance; a number of them continue to this day. They are often serious and involve dramatic adventures. Strips such as *Little Orphan Annie* and *Dick Tracy* are not comic at all, and their preoccupation with man's supposedly evil nature, with crime and murder, reflect just how quickly our innocence dissipated after the World War I.

This period—from 1920 to 1960—has been described by George E. Mowry in *The Urban Nation*. He mentions two important developments which gave the period its character—the change from a rural to an urban nation, and the development of a mass production-consumption society. He describes the first matter as follows:

> Sometime between 1915 and 1920 the old rural majority living on the producing land, or close to it in small towns and villages, became a minority. The changes resulting from this transformation from a rural to an urban nation were to be just as momentous as those that had accompanied the conversion of the frontier into a settled land.

This rural majority was comprised for the most part of white Anglo-Saxon Protestants, most of whom "believed in self-help, hard work, thrift, and personal sobriety. They disliked bigness, diversity, the exotic, leisure, elegance, and personal indulgence." These people, Mowry suggests, held onto the "agrarian myth" even after they abandoned the farm and came to the city.

When they did come to the city, however, they found themselves assaulted by another revolutionary development:

> The rapid evolution during the twenties of the "ad mass," or the mass-production-consumption society, tied together big business and the masses in a symbiotic relationship so close that the health of one was the health of the other. By developing new techniques and institutions necessary to bind the consuming crowd to the corporate board room this new type of economic society also sapped and destroyed in daily practice much of the content of the rural creed, though verbal and emotional commitment to the old values continued to be celebrated in many social rites.

Indeed! We find vestiges of the old values in some of the strips of the period, just as we will find a repudiation of these values as we move toward the sixties and the post-modern comics.

Some of the more important comics of the period are:

HAROLD GRAY, *Little Orphan Annie,* 1924
HAM FISCHER, *Joe Palooka,* 1927
WALT DISNEY, *Mickey Mouse,* 1928
ELZIE SEGAR, *Popeye,* 1929
PHIL NOWLAND, *Buck Rogers,* 1929
HAROLD FOSTER, *Tarzan,* 1929
CHIC YOUNG, *Blondie,* 1930
CHESTER GOULD, *Dick Tracy,* 1931
ALEX RAYMOND, *Flash Gordon,* 1933
MILTON CANIFF, *Terry and the Pirates,* 1934
AL CAPP, *Li'l Abner,* 1934
HAROLD FOSTER, *Prince Valiant,* 1937
J. SIEGEL and J. SHUSTER, *Superman,* 1938
BOB KANE, *Batman,* 1939
WALT KELLY, *Pogo,* 1948
CHARLES SCHULZ, *Peanuts,* 1950

The list could be extended with scores—even hundreds—of names, but the ones mentioned above are certainly the major strips and heroic figures of the era. Few of them, it can be seen, are humorous; and even some of the funny ones —as I have tried to demonstrate—deal with issues of the most serious nature, though masked in a veneer of comic inanity.

A glance at the list of most important strips of the age of innocence and the modern age comics shows the remark able changes which took place in American society and culture. To the extent that comic strips and comic books (and all forms of the high arts and popular arts) reflect the society from which they spring, we find, in just a few years, some incredible changes though a remarkable kind of continuity in other respects. *The Yellow Kid,* for example, presages the urban age, and reflects, a generation before its time, the shape of things to come. In the same way, *Buck Rogers* previewed the seventies in the thirties. Both, however, sprang from a Calvinist view of man which saw him as unregenerate and depraved—which we might expect in a culture influenced so strongly by the Puritans.

The final break with Puritanism comes with the postmodern comics, but more on this later.

LITTLE ORPHAN ANNIE
The Abandoned Years

Much has been written about Gray's free-swinging conservatism, and it is quite true that he has advanced his own views in the strip. His editorializing begins, however, not with flat statements about rationing, taxes or freedom of enterprise, but in his very cast of characters. The pattern of piety and virtue is not simply a literary convention; it is a reflection of the belief that the good life is the patient, unassuming, well-ordered life. Within that pattern lie safety, happiness and the good society; outside it lie danger and evil, corruption and damnation.
— STEPHEN BECKER, *Comic Art in America*

. . . Little Orphan Annie and her friends support the status quo and in some respects would prefer to go back to the good old days. Orphan Annie approves the symbols which have traditionally represented good in our society and she condemns some of the well-known sins. Actually, she reflects the conservative social idealism of the middle class in our society. The strip emphasizes reliance on "providence," faith,

hope and charity—but not too much charity. If people need help, let it be voluntary aid from their neighbors and associates, and not forced by the law. Orphan Annie is for the church, truth, hard work, and pressure when necessary in order to get what one wants. She opposes crooks, politicians, slowness in government, and foreigners who would like U.S. military secrets.
—LYLE W. SHANNON, *Public Opinion Quarterly.*

Little Orphan Annie is a legacy of the Coolidge era. The strip started in 1924 and continues to this day, though Harold Gray, its creator, died recently. How much longer it will continue remains to be seen, for it is an anachronism, speaking to a generation that is dying out also. One of the conventions of the comic strip is that its heroes do not age (though there are few exceptions to this notion). Not only has Annie not aged—she is still a tiny waif after fifty years of fantastic adventures—but she has not changed.

Gray has faithfully been promulgating a philosophy that seemed valid when he started, but which time and events have rendered obsolete. In a sense, then, Annie's vacant eyes are significant. They do not see American society as it is, but seem to be focused on a society that existed fifty years ago. And even then, there is good reason to believe that Gray was nostalgic for a world that never was, a world of homely virtue and small-town, rural values, of respect for tradition and authority.

Introduced at a time when "the business of America is business" was the prevailing social philosophy, it was only logical that the hero of the strip should be a benevolent capitalist. He is a figure of world importance who is involved in intrigues which involve nothing less than the sur-

GEE, "DADDY"— IS IT REALLY TRUE? WILL EONITE DO ALL THE THINGS THEY CLAIM?

YES, ANNIE— IT WILL REVOLUTIONIZE THE CIVILIZED WORLD— IT'S TRANSPARENT AS GLASS, BUT WILL TAKE ANY COLOR— IT'S MANY TIMES STRONGER THAN STEEL—

7-5

NEITHER ACID, HEAT, TIME NOR WEATHER AFFECTS EONITE IN THE LEAST— EONITE WILL BE USED TO REPLACE EVERY THING BUILT OR USED BY MAN, FROM BUILDINGS TO DISHES—

ELI SAYS A TOY CANNON MADE OF EONITE WOULD SHOOT THIRTY MILES—

PROBABLY— THE NATION WHICH POSSESSES EONITE WILL HAVE NOTHING TO FEAR FROM FOREIGN FOES—

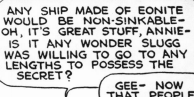

ANY SHIP MADE OF EONITE WOULD BE NON-SINKABLE— OH, IT'S GREAT STUFF, ANNIE— IS IT ANY WONDER SLUGG WAS WILLING TO GO TO ANY LENGTHS TO POSSESS THE SECRET?

GEE— NOW THAT PEOPLE KNOW ABOUT IT, OTHER FOLKS WILL WANT IT, TOO—

HAROLD GRAY

vival of the United States and, associated with this, freedom. He is not presented as an awesome figure. In fact, he is made rather ordinary by assuming the title "daddy." There is an ambiguity in this term: it could either mean a "big daddy" or boss, or it could mean an affectionate term for father. The point is that by calling Oliver Warbucks "daddy," he is humanized and made to seem rather ordinary, though we see him involved with other matters that are far removed from that kind of pose.

His last name, Warbucks, is indicative of the source of his money—he is literally a war profiteer. However, the source of his fabulous wealth is not a major consideration. True to the ideals of the Gospel of Wealth, which he exemplifies, he is a servant of mankind, and his fabulous wealth imposes upon him responsibility for moral stewardship of the highest order. The aura of mystery and fantasy that pervade his actions in the strip, and those of his servants Asp and Punjab, suggest that some kind of higher law is at work in the beneficent selection of creative and heroic men such as Warbucks. In a world whose law is competition for survival (as the social Darwinists believed), those at the top are, by definition, the most fit, the best. Success is an indication of merit, harkening back to the Puritan ethic.

Little Orphan Annie exemplifies all of this conservative political philosophy—which sees the good society created by competing individuals in a laissez-faire ambience. Annie cannot explain how the good society can be achieved by the selfishness of each individual, and can only rail in bitterness at the society in which she finds herself—urban, complicated, cosmopolitan, and bureaucratic.

It is Annie's function to show Americans that there is a way, that all is not lost, and it is her tragic fate that nobody (to speak of) will listen to her. In the introduction to a collection of the strip, entitled *Arf! The Life and Hard Times of Little Orphan Annie (1935-1945),* Al Capp tells of his meeting with Gray a number of years ago:

> He said: "I know your stuff, Capp. You're going to be around a long time. Take my advice and buy a house in the country. Build a wall around it. And get ready to protect yourself. The way things are going, people who earn their living someday are going to have to fight off the bums."

This quote reveals a number of themes which inform the strip—a sense of isolation on the part of the virtuous; a reverence for nature and the country, where life is simple and honest; a sense that one's fate is in one's own hands and that salvation involves a retreat to enclaves of virtue and a repudiation of the evil way of the world in general.

These are traditional American ideas relating directly to our Puritan heritage and the desire to escape from the decadence of European society to the natural wilderness of America, where individuals could fashion their own simple and natural societies and lead the good life. This concept came to a focus in the Jacksonian period. When the American repudiates Europe he becomes an orphan like Annie, though a cultural one. He is free then, to create himself without the burden of a past, without the burden of institutions, and traditions. From this point of view the price of freedom is loneliness. Into this paradise of innocence and

nature slides the serpent of European ideas, such as social-
ism and government spending, and all kinds of evil figures
from foreign lands who seek to destroy America by encour-
aging dissent or stealing secrets.

In such a situation Daddy Warbucks finds himself
somewhat of a loner amongst people who have been corrupted and have lost the old virtues. His mission is to prevent evil from triumphing in America, and the general de-
basement of American society makes it possible for his
activities to assume heroic proportions, at least in the eyes
of those sympathetic to his goals. He is aided in his work by
two mysterious Orientals, both of whom are killers. They
have a license to kill, so to speak, since it is always for a
good cause.

Little Orphan Annie is a morality play dealing with the
preservation of American innocence and democracy and
based on the myth of the chosen few. It is ironic that this
myth is believed by both radicals of the right and the left.
This matter is explained in Mircea Eliade's *Sacred and
Profane:*

> Marx takes over and continues one of the great eschatological
> myths of the Asiatico-Mediterranean world—the redeeming
> role of the Just (the "chosen," the "anointed," the "in-
> nocent," the "messenger"; in our day, the proletariat), whose
> sufferings are destined to change the ontological status of the
> world. In fact, Marx's classless society and the consequent
> disappearance of historical tensions find their closest prece-
> dent in the myth of the Golden Age that many traditions put
> at the beginning and the end of history.

Annie and her friends, then, are modern inheritors of this

myth and will redeem American society by pointing out where the danger lies. It is a prolonged jeremiad calling people to their senses—asking for a return to the good old days, though it refuses to acknowledge the great crash and depression, which destroyed America's faith in the businessman as a culture hero and in the moral superiority of the businessman.

Warbucks always argues that redtape, and a well-meaning but destructive governmental bureaucracy, is what prevents him from succeeding in his various tasks. At times, also, Warbucks merges into other roles, such as that of the military hero, in which case he takes on an astonishing resemblance to General Eisenhower.* In the May 4 and May 5, 1942, strips we find Daddy Warbucks in military uniform with three stars, a lieutenant general, no less —except that he does not have a U.S. on his uniform. We are to infer that he has some kind of a "special position" and are told he has a *secret mission* on a very high level, since he is involved with diplomats and others who prevent him from fighting.

These strips exemplify the same kind of attitudes found in all paramilitary organizations (usually associated with right-wing political beliefs). The government is stuck in red tape and perhaps even infiltrated by traitors. In such a case direct action is called for, even if it is not strictly legal. The dilemma is one that most of these groups refuse to recognize: how do you justify lawlessness in the name of

* There is an obvious Oedipal aspect to Dodds "Warbucks" role, just as Eisenhower was seen as a kind of father figure. Warbucks, like "Ike" is also a good Joe, and an excellent representative of democratic capitalism—a trillionaire who is not snotty and snobbish.

preserving "law and order"?

We also find in *Little Orphan Annie* the same kind of diffuse paranoia common to paramilitary groups—a sense that the enemy is everywhere, and that none (except for a certain few) can be trusted. Annie continually falls into the hands of spies and dangerous characters, who are intent upon destroying America, and with it, freedom, free enterprise, capitalism, and benevolent billionaires such as Daddy Warbucks. All of this is tied to the notion that history is a record of great men (on various kinds of secret missions) fighting secret conspiracies, which attempt to despoil an essentially good society. If these conspiracies can be thwarted, then the natural goodness of the society can manifest itself and flourish.

In many respects Harold Gray is an agitator, as defined by Leo Lowenthal and Norbert Guterman in their study *Prophets of Deceit*. In this content analysis of the techniques of American agitators, Lowenthal and Guterman discovered certain recurrent motifs, what they call *the constants of agitation*, which express certain predispositions in the audiences of the agitator. They explain it as follows:

> Agitation may be viewed as a specific type of public activity and the agitator as a specific type of "advocate of social change"—a concept that will serve us as a convenient frame of reference.

> The immediate cause of the activity of an "advocate of social change" is a social condition that a section of the population feels to be iniquitous or frustrating. This discontent he articulates by pointing out its presumed causes. He proposes to defeat the social groups held responsible for perpetuating the

social condition that gives rise to discontent. Finally, he promotes a movement capable of achieving this objective and
proposes himself as its leader.

Gray does not, of course, go quite this far, but his strip
reflects a kind of malaise afflicting society and he does indicate the direction in which he feels society should move.

Central themes in the agitator's message, according to
Lowenthal and Guterman, are The Eternal Dupes, The Corrupt Government, The Reds, and The Bullet Proof Martyr,
as well as The Conspiracy. All have obvious relevance to
Little Orphan Annie. It may seem somewhat harsh to suggest that a number of the themes found in a comic strip
have dangerous implications, but even real agitators are
often unaware of the import of their message. As Lowenthal
and Guterman point out:

> How conscious the agitator is of the genuine meaning of his
> message is a moot question that we have not attempted to
> answer here. . . . But for the purpose of finding the inner
> meaning and recurrent patterns of agitation, the presence or
> absence of consciousness on the part of the agitators is ul-
> timately of secondary importance.

> In any case, the distinction between the manifest and latent
> meaning of an agitational text must be seen as crucial. Taken
> at their face value, agitational texts seem merely as an indul-
> gence in futile furies about vague disturbances. Translated
> into their psychological equivalents, agitational texts are
> seen as consistent, meaningful, and significantly related to
> the social world.

There is a certain old-fashioned campy charm to the

strip and its innocent revelation of racism and bigotry—but in part it was the mood of the times that Gray reflected. In 1945 it was perfectly all right to call Japanese people "Japs," and Germans "Krauts," as Annie did in the comics. The times have changed, fortunately. Gray died in 1968, but the strip continues, though without the same *élan.* A statement he once made explains a great deal about the strip:

> Annie will continue to sell the idea that life is a battle, and victory for the brave and stronghearted alone. Probably she'll never grasp complete victory, but she'll get a few tail feathers now and then.

Gray seems to recognize that the politics of normalcy and the rural, small-town, nativistic values he held dear were an anachronism, but he could not give them up.

Marshall McLuhan sees the strip as dealing with the success myth in America (*Mechanical Bride*):

> In her isolation and feminine "helplessness" Harold Gray has portrayed for millions of readers the central success drama of America—that of the young, committed to the rejection of parents, that they may justify both the parents and themselves.

This is a valuable insight, since it helps explain the aura of despair and desperation which permeates the strip, and which shows itself in all the poor, humble, and frustrated folk who populate it. Gray never entertains the notion that a society which produces such types may itself be guilty in some way; instead he brings in bogeymen of all sorts who serve as scapegoats. In a very real sense *Little Orphan Annie* reflects the failure of one of the central organizing myths of American culture, the myth of success, the so-called American Dream; the tragedy is that Gray is so intoxicated by illusion that he refuses to see reality or acknowledge history. In that sense the tragedy of Little Orphan Annie is the tragedy of millions of Americans who live, like Annie, in a nightmare world and cannot recognize it, though they may feel it somehow and are forced to seek relief in fantasies of childhood.

But what is it that is disturbing all the ordinary folk in the strip and the ordinary folk who read it? Aside from what Daddy Warbucks stands for in relation to the various intrigues in *Little Orphan Annie,* he has another dimension that is worth considering. Transcendent heroes (who loom high above the ordinary man) by their very stature reveal the pettiness and triviality of the common man. And thus, by contrasting our lot with his, Warbucks makes us aware of our own alienation.

Alienation may be impossible to define satisfactorily, but is something we have all felt, and still feel, even if we have difficulty pinning the term down. It has to do with being a cipher (or at least feeling like one) and having nothing individual or personal about oneself; it involves a sense of being estranged (from others and from oneself) and a sense of powerlessness, anonymity, and insignificance. Thus

Warbucks's heroics and the fact that we *need* his heroics serves to point out our weakness, inadequacy, and powerlessness.

Polls taken in America suggest that large numbers of people here are leading lives of quiet desperation for one reason or another. Many people have jobs that are unsatisfying. Others have trouble with their children, problems with alcohol or drugs, or with their marriage. Some poor souls have compounds of most or all of these afflictions. The ordinary man has become a victim of a culture that has, to a great extent, lost sight of personal and humane values and which now measures everyone against one standard: how much money do you make? The ordinary man has become the "affordinary man," a person whose only distinction is what he can afford. (*Afford:* to be able to bear the cost of without serious loss or detriment.) Warbucks, by virtue of his vast wealth is in a realm beyond our fondest hopes. He is in with the "big boys," his actions have a world-historical dimension, and he can afford *anything*.

All of our distinctions—a sense of humor, courage, honesty, kindness—have been replaced by our buying powers and the ironic thing is that we have been taught to measure our progress (affordinancy) by our dehumanization. This is a function of our equalitarian society, in which there are no official or legal class distinctions. We do not have a hereditary aristocracy (*aristoi* means best), and so the only way a person can show he has made it is by conspicuous consumption. You are what you can afford.

But though we do not have an official social aristocracy, we have an economic one. Those in the highest strata of society, a bare one percent of the population, lead relatively private and privileged lives, and as a result of intermarriage, etc., our economic aristocracy becomes, in effect, a social one also. But it is not legal or official, so that many Americans delude themselves into thinking that we have no classes. Although there are some opportunities for social mobility, those at the top start out way ahead and very few are able to catch up with them.

Since we measure achievement in economic terms, those at the bottom of the socioeconomic ladder suffer from a grievous sense of inadequacy, and perhaps frustration. It is in this situation that Daddy Warbucks works his magic, for *his role for the common man is to act as an apologist for corporate capitalism, to show that those at the top deserve to be there and are needed for their special abilities.* Warbucks's mysterious adventures serve to *mystify* the ordinary man, who is "let in" on the notion that Warbucks is making significant decisions and actions which serve to protect democracy and freedom. To attack Warbucks is, then, ultimately to attack democracy, and to risk annihilation at the hands of Punjab or Asp.

Once the equation of Warbucks (or capitalism) and democracy is made, Warbucks moves beyond criticism, for he is a savior and the ultimate goodness of his ends justify the occasional brutality (by his henchmen) of his acts. An example of Warbucks's linkage to democracy can be seen in a recent episode in the strip, done by Gray's successor and imitator, Philip Blaisdell (April 27, 1969). Warbucks is having a conversation with a counterfeiting wizard named Dr. Zzyz. Zzyz shows Warbucks a dove, symbol of peace, which

he then turns into an adder. He says, "You have been deceived, capitalist Warbucks, and to the deceiver belongs the
spoils!!" Warbucks grabs the adder and smashes it to death
against the wall, replying, "We may slip a little, even stum-
ble and lose our way sometimes . . . but we've got a *built-
in-compass* that keeps pointing the way to the *greatest good
for the greatest number* . . . it's called *'democracy'* and if
you can't *beat* it, don't *knock* it!!" Capitalist Warbucks,
the great utilitarian, has spoken, and the message is that
capitalism is directly related to democracy and that capitalists do have a socially redeeming function.

Blaisdell does not have Gray's talents and the message
that *Little Orphan Annie* has to tell the American public is
now rather hard to swallow. Daddy Warbucks has, all of a
sudden, become irrelevant to people, and this fact suggests
that major changes are occurring in the political conscious-
ness of the American public, changes which will have an
important role in determining the shape of our society in
the future.

BUCK ROGERS

The New Renaissance Hero of the Space Epics

Buck Rogers is the first of the great American space operas in comic-strip form. It achieved immense popularity rather quickly, from the date of its appearance, on January 7, 1929, and held its appeal until 1967, when it ended. Set in the twenty-fifth century, it gave its creators the chance to indulge in all manner of fantastic futuristic exploits: they created strange vehicles that anticipated our modern rockets; they evolved all manner of remarkable weapons and manipulated the laws of nature in bizarre ways. This was done with so much flair and imagination that *Buck Rogers* is, today, synonymous with futuristic technological creations, and is defined in *Webster's Third International Dictionary* as such.

It is technology that is romanticized in *Buck Rogers,* not science *per se.* "Scientists often" must work to save the world from foreign invaders, but their work involves creating weapons that Buck and his friends can use. In this respect, *Buck Rogers* is a rather faithful mirror of basic American values (for we have developed a remarkable technology and seem more interested in practical applications of the laws of science than basic research) and a picture of what was to come in America (for we have created the most fantastic panoply of weapons known in the history of man).

Technology, of course, is not *all* that is needed. It is necessary, but not sufficient! There is, as in most American comics, a stress on heroism and bravery—on the human dimension. Often, as a matter of fact, the enemy has superior technology, but because he is deficient in will and is cowardly, he loses. In 1929, when *Buck Rogers* appeared, the notion of the self-made man and belief in the supreme efficacy of will power and determination were just beginning to crumble. These beliefs would never totally disappear, though events such as the stock market crash and the depression would seriously modify the value we place on individual initiative.

The will-to-riches and success motif had been dominant here, permeating our children's literature. The best known examples of these, the Horatio Alger novels, stopped early in the twentieth century, but the values and beliefs championed by Alger lingered, and were then caught up in comics, which took the ball and ran from where Alger had left it. It is not surprising, then, to see heroism and particularly *will* emphasized in *Buck Rogers* and in many of the other comics which followed. These notions are, after all, central facets in the American belief system.

The picture of the twenty-fifth century we find in Buck Rogers is not at all pleasant. If there were great anxieties in America in 1929, they certainly manifested themselves in *Buck Rogers,* for we have a horrendous anti-utopia or dystopia, in which civilization as we know it has been destroyed and men are locked in combat with all kinds of menacing aliens and grotesque figures. Many of these aliens are Oriental, and when the World War II starts we find a great deal of thinly disguised anti-Japanese propaganda, reflecting, no doubt, the prevalent sentiments of the time. (This anti-Japanese propaganda was also reflected in the cinema, which had leering Japanese generals always lusting for white American women.)

In addition to these villains, there were *homunculae*— little men called asterites; there were also half-breed humans who roamed the wildernesses of a devastated North America, and villainous turncoats, with one in particular, Buck's nemesis, "Killer Kane." Much of the action is motivated by love, curiously enough. Buck Rogers is often forced into adventures to rescue his beloved Wilma from some enemy villain who has captured her. In addition, we find a considerable amount of sexual jealousy in the plots, as a sideline to the basic problem of gaining power and keeping it, or saving the world from destruction.

Man has scattered into various enclaves and is in the process of rebuilding civilization in the face of opposition by Martians and other kinds of barbarians. In a sense, *Buck Rogers* carries the historical cycle of destruction and rebirth

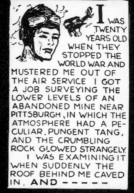

a step further. The destruction of Rome in the fifth century, by the barbarians, is simply moved up two millenia, and the rebirth (literally renaissance) of man is retold in a different setting.

The central question, however, is the same one: *military technology and its social and political consequences.* The only constant seems to be human nature, the ultimate weapon. For the aliens who have destroyed civilization and who constantly threaten the second renaissance are intelligent, but they are deficient (as we might expect) in the human virtues—generosity, kindness, affection, love, and patriotism. Thus, like the barbarians who overthrew the Holy Roman Empire, they are doomed. After all, the strip was written and illustrated by men who were socialized in America and were writing for a large American audience which knew that virtue always wins in the last analysis.

What Americans have always suspected is now shown to be true: civilization and all the generous human values that go with it can only be reborn in the American wilderness. The new history of man starts in America with American heroes. Foreigners, strangers, those who look different (the Orientals), or who have not accepted American values (the half-breeds and other kinds of "degenerates") present a danger. This danger will be met by heroic technologists and brave men who are willing to risk their lives for their beliefs.

Aside from the incredible technological aspects of the strip, it is rather amateurishly drawn and written. Neither the art work, which is quite crude, nor the plots, which are

Dick Calkins, who did the art work, nor Phil Nowlan, who took over the continuity in 1934, was a really first-rate creative artist, and *Buck Rogers,* despite its action and violence, is rather boring. As Stephen Becker wrote in *Comic Art in America:*

> The strip itself is a study in "pioneering"—as the first of the science-fiction strips, it now seems overmelodramatic, drawn plainly and simply, and even—strangely enough—slightly unimaginative. But its impact during the thirties was powerful, and it led the way for many imitations and variations.

One reason for the strip's popularity in the thirties is its seeming optimism—for the theme of the strip is man's ability to transcend what seem to be the most difficult problems. To people suffering during the depression, the notion that civilization could be rebuilt was a source of comfort. What was not obvious was that the strip, despite its futurism, was quite reactionary—identifying progress as a function of individual initiative. It was the blind American faith in individualism and our worship of that arch-individualist, the robber baron, which had landed us in the mess in which we found ourselves. And the solution we were offered in *Buck Rogers,* though we didn't recognize it, was more of the same. We dressed our hero up in futuristic space garb and equipped him with ray guns and other paraphernalia, but the theme remained the same: redemption by the heroic individual.

Quite likely, *Buck Rogers* is significant because it signals an unconscious recognition of the ultimate meaning of technology for American society. It may even be that the rather flat, dead character of the strip is a reflection of the impact of technology on man's psyche—the matter-of-factness, mechanization, repetition, and invariability of the machines, pursuing a logic of their own, not only shape but tend to overwhelm man and society.

In this sense, *Buck Rogers* deals with the human spirit in conflict with the natural forces of machines and technology. The implicit threat lurking in the shadows of *Buck Rogers* is that of natural forces capturing man. The very setting of the strip, a devastated world organized around the principle of avoiding Martian warships and other instruments of destruction, points this out.

A generation before *Buck Rogers* appeared, Henry Adams had recognized the meaning of technology and speculated about it in *The Education of Henry Adams*. In his chapter "The Dynamo and the Virgin" he sensed the significance of technology in The Great Exposition of 1900. Adams saw the dynamos in the exhibition as having a moral force, and, indeed, moral imperatives. As he wrote:

> Before the end, one began to pray to it; inherited instinct taught the natural expression of man before silent and infinite force. Among the thousand symbols of ultimate energy, the dynamo was not so human as some, but it was the most expressive.

The dynamo has given way to the space ship, but the same dynamics apply to both.

Buck Rogers is an adventure in "technological radicalism and social conservatism," to borrow a phrase from Philip Slater's *The Pursuit of Loneliness*. Conservatism is actually, in this case, too mild a term. We have a kind of reactionary militaristic society based on the notion of heroic individualism which is subservient to the imperatives of the machines, though this notion is not recognized. It is one of the great ironies that a strip which has tended to be characterized as a magnificent kind of adventure of the human spirit is, in fact, a study of man one step removed from robotism and totalitarianism.

BLONDIE
The Irrelevance of the American Husband

Blondie was one of the most popular, if not the most popular, American comic strips until the meteoric rise of *Peanuts* in recent years. Its subject is an American family, and it presents a rather depressing image of our conception of the American husband. Dagwood Bumstead, as many commentators have pointed out, is an infantile, weak, greedy, and incompetent figure. As Marshall McLuhan put it, in *The Mechanical Bride:*

> Dagwood is a supernumerary tooth with weak hams and a cuckold hair-do . . . is seedy, baggy, bewildered and weakly dependent. . . . He is an apologetic intruder into a hygienic,

and save for himself, a well-ordered dormitory. His attempts to eke out some sort of existence in the bathroom or the sofa (face to the wall) are always promptly challenged. He is a joke which his children thoroughly understand. He has failed but Alexander will succeed.

McLuhan sees Dagwood as assuming a little-boy role under the pressure of Blondie's mothering wedlock, and goes on to relate the strip to Margaret Mead's theory that the third generation in America is the one that will succeed.

Others have commented similarly on *Blondie.* Geoffrey Gorer, in *The American People,* said, "Although naturally exaggerated, Dagwood does represent a very widely spread attitude toward the American man as husband and father. Dagwood is kind, dutiful, diligent, well-meaning within his limits: but he has so completely given up any claim to authority that the family would constantly risk disintegration and disaster, if it were not for Blondie." This attitude toward the American male has, in recent years, crystallized in the disappearance of fathers from situation comedies on television, or, in some cases, of mothers. Having a missing father makes romance more possible while it allows the domestic comedy to continue.

Dagwood Bumstead represents an important archetype in the American psyche—the irrelevant male. He is still in the strip, but he is only there as an object of ridicule and a symbol of inadequacy and stupidity. His job was breeding, and now that that is done with, and Alexander and Cookie produced, he remains on as a fool, and the butt of many jokes.

His name is absurd, the name of an irrelevant person, a

clown. Bumstead is silly: perhaps it is close to bump and to lump, which suggests, perhaps, *lumpenproletariat.* Bum also means tramp and rear end, neither of which are flattering. (Strange to think that the offspring of this nothing would be named Alexander, the name of a world conqueror.) His face, with those two dots for eyes and the hair standing out in two tufts, as if they were horns and he were cuckolded, is ludicrous, and even more so since Blondie is relatively realistically drawn, often with a good bit of leg showing. Actually Dagwood's face has changed from the first strips; when he was a rich young man he was portrayed more realistically. Now, with the cuckold hairdo, he represents an ancient tradition in comedy: the man whose wife has been unfaithful to him but who is unaware of it. This humor is based on exposure and ignorance—we know something Dagwood doesn't. And Dagwood's general inadequacy at the job and around the house fits in well with the notion that he is probably inadequate in the bedroom.

Since he has no sex life, he gains his satisfaction through gluttony. The kind of sandwich he made famous, the Dagwood sandwich, is a hodgepodge of leftovers in the refrigerator all wedged in between two slices of bread. Food seems to be his only real source of gratification, which suggests that he is a case of arrested development, never having left the oral stage for the genital. In that sense, he is a child himself, and assuming the little-boy role should not be very difficult for him.

There are, of course, certain limitations necessitated by the domestic comedy. The sources of humor must be relatively obvious, tied to family doings, and over seemingly harmless and trivial events. But beneath the lightheaded and rather simple-minded humor of the strip, which uses exaggeration and error as two basic modes of operation, there is the theme of the irrelevant male who is an object of humiliation. Dagwood has been disinherited, is browbeaten by a domineering and assertive wife, is abused by his boss, and is generally a failure in everything he tries, although his intentions are often generous.

The fact that *Blondie* got started in the height of the depression may have some significance. It was a period when our faith in the businessman was just beginning to founder, when many were in the midst of terrible hardships, and when the average workingman, still imbued with the self-made man myth, saw himself as ultimately responsible for his dire predicament. It has been suggested, in fact, that the comics filled the inspirational gap left by the decline of the Horatio Alger story.

Dagwood's decline, then, mirrors a sense of inadequacy and irrelevance and, in particular, powerlessness, that was quite widespread in American society. After his fall from power as the son of a rich man to a disinherited, castrated family man, he takes on the semblance of a clown. His life is one of continual ignominious defeat, masked by a thin veneer of geniality and slapstick buffoonery. But there he is: a man who hates his job, is abused by his wife, and is the butt of a thousand jokes. There is almost a heroic dimension to Dagwood Bumstead—he refuses to be destroyed —but he is not truly heroic because he lacks self-awareness and self-understanding. Thus he is pathetic, not tragic.

An early strip is most instructive. Dagwood introduces

his fiancée, Blondie, to his father. He brings her to his father's office. The father says, "But son I'm awfully busy . . . I'm working out plans for this new merger." Dagwood says, "But Pop . . . I want you to meet Blondie . . . we're engaged you know . . . This is Blondie, Dad—she's awfully bashful and shy . . . you'll love her." Blondie says, "Oh tee hee . . . I always feel so boo-boop-a-doop when I meet my boyfriends' papas. . . . *But I usually like them better than the sons.* . . . [My emphasis.] Can't I call you "Pop," Mr. Bumstead? Tee-hee." Dagwood says that they have to leave so as to give his father time to work out his plans for his "new merger." Blondie responds "Oh Pop . . . if you aren't the terror! What are you going to do with your old wife?" She has misinterpreted what Dagwood meant by "merger," which is the source of the humor in this day's strip. There is a certain element of aggression in the phrase "old wife" and a hint of what is to come in marriage with her revelation that she likes her boyfriends' fathers better than their sons.

In this early strip, Dagwood is a young playboy-type who seems to lack any notion of what is in store for him when he is married. A look at Dagwood in later episodes shows an entirely different scene—the one we are familiar with—which is based on the notion that marriage is debilitating and destructive of virility and masculinity. This has now become a veritable cliché in the comics and in popular culture in general. (Charles Winick has pointed out that romantic love in advertisements seldom involves marriage partners; it takes place during courtship and amongst single people.)

Dagwood's attempts to retreat are also futile. He takes

to the sofa, with his face hidden from the reader, in an attempt to find a bit of peace and quiet, some solitude. But these attempts are not successful. He cannot evade Blondie's dominance. The relationship between Dagwood and Blondie is a parody of that existing in many families, in which there is a domineering figure who tends to do the decision making (and "holds the marriage together") and a passive figure who is acted upon, subservient, and submissive. Except that it does not seem possible for this kind of a relationship to exist without various attempts, on the part of the passive figure, to assert himself, gain some kind of psychic equilibrium and, perhaps, in some subversive way, control things.

Dagwood's inadequacy is a form of control, for Blondie must take care of things, run the house, solve the problems, do whatever has to be done. What we find in Dagwood is a form of "aggressive passivity" that he uses as a tool of domination. This aggressive passivity takes a number of forms, such as Dagwood's not doing certain things that are expected of him, and his being overwhelmed and rendered incapable of doing things, and his refusal to acknowledge what is expected of him and, thus, remaining free not to act. It is a form of control by weakness and purposive inadequacy.

If Dagwood Bumstead is an irrelevant male, a bumbling fool who cannot be counted upon to do anything adequately, it is, in part, because he "chooses to be so at great cost to his sense of self and self-esteem." In a sense he has made Blondie into what she is. In many families the same tragic pattern of active and passive aggression is repeated, with disastrous results all around. In this respect, Blondie is

as much sinned against as sinner, and her mothering wedlock is not entirely a matter of her own choosing, as is the
case in many families.

The widespread popularity of the strip signifies, I believe, some kind of a subliminal awareness on the part of
the readers of *Blondie*'s actual relevance. *Blondie* is the
most popular comic strip of domestic relations in America,
and one reason for this is that the readers can see beneath
the humor and recognize their own patterns of behavior
being acted out, even if this is done in a highly exaggerated
and zany manner. The humor, after all, is often quite bland
and not particularly effective. Thus it is unlikely that the
humor of each strip is what interests readers. The probabil-
ity is, rather, that the representation of pathetic domestic
relations cloaked in exaggeration and absurdity really intrigues us. In *Comic Art in America*, Stephen Becker says
that Dagwood "wins" about fifteen percent of the time.
This is not a very good batting average, but is necessary to
maintain a mild element of suspense. The basic question
we ask ourselves when we read *Blondie* is—how will Dagwood be ridiculed? We know what to expect; we don't know
how it will be done.

It may be that one of Dagwood's functions for us, as
readers, involves his inadequacy, which makes us so much
superior. He reassures us, in a sense, that we are not alone
and not as bad as some. And in the strip we are allowed to
watch with fascination a low-keyed (in terms of awareness
on the part of the participants) enactment of our own domestic tribulations and tragedies. Dagwood is irrelevant
because he has no interiority, no soul, and no adequately

developed male identity. He is shown in one episode as nothing but a source of money for Blondie, who goes on a spending jag. Perhaps one of the reasons for Dagwood's plight, aside from the fact that contemporary American society offers no adequately delineated male identity, is that he is so good-natured and willing, at all times, to see the humor in situations. He even makes light of his being mined by Blondie—because he has been taught, like all of us, to be a good Joe.

This pose of good-naturedness reflects an unwillingness to face problems, to become angry or upset. It is one of the basic role-myths in American culture to be cheerful and to avoid showing how you really feel. What happens, ultimately, is that the pose takes over and we lose the capacity to feel or, at least, to admit our feelings to ourselves. This, in turn, leads to the repression of feelings which, in real people, often manifest themselves in destructive ways.

Many American males are currently struggling with the problem of attaining a usable male identity. As the Marlboro advertisements show, we still tend to see the male as a rough and tough figure from the frontier—a heritage of the past—which does not help much since we are now an urbanized and bureaucratic society, and one in which there is a great deal of desexualization going on. (This is the argument of Charles Winick in *The New People*.) The situation becomes exacerbated when you have the men (and the women) locked in the kind of familiar relationship portrayed in Blondie.

Dagwood Bumstead lacks ego strength. He does not recognize the damage that is being done to him (or has been done to him) owing to his notion of how he should conduct himself and how he should relate to his wife and children. Exploited (and exploiting, in his own subtle way), abused, depersonalized, and all but destroyed (in great part because of a fear of rejection), Dagwood is in the tragic situation of being an irrelevant male, and feeling it, but not knowing it. To the extent that he is an archetype for American men, who find that many of the situations in the strip some- how "strike a chord," it is a tragedy of the most profound dimensions.

DICK TRACY

The Avenger—
Evangelical Protestant Style

Interestingly enough, in retrospect we can see that the most profound insights into American society were in the popular art of the Thirties, the gangster films and the detective novels. These were grim and despairing portrayals of dehumanization, violence, and the bleakness of the American city. The remarkable novels of Raymond Chandler, James M. Cain, and Dashiell Hammett come closer to the truth than almost anything else in literature or social science. And on the screen or in the newspapers, the gangster era gave America a grotesque portrait of itself, with the whole economic and social system cruelly displayed for those who would and could see it.
— CHARLES A. REICH, *The Greening of America*

There is a famous story about the distinguished cartoonist Charles Addams (probably apocryphal) to the effect that he "cracks up" every once in a while, and always announces it by sending a certain cartoon to *The New Yorker*. The cartoon shows one of Addams's weird characters in a maternity-ward waiting room. He says to the nurse, who brings his newborn baby, "Don't bother wrapping it—I'll eat it here." One wonders what kind of a cartoon Gould would draw if he cracked up, because his famous comic strip, *Dick Tracy,* is so permeated by grotesques and monsters that it would take an imagination of colossal proportions to outdo his everyday fantasy.

The origins of *Dick Tracy* explain in part certain characteristics of the strip. In a recent collection sampling the first twenty years of Dick Tracy, an excellent introduction by Ellery Queen sheds light on the strip: Chester Gould, *The Celebrated Cases of Dick Tracy (1931-1951)*, Chelsea House, 1970. Queen characterizes the American society which spawned *Dick Tracy* as one of recklessness, lawlessness, and violence, bred in part by the depression. Queen believes that Dick Tracy, whose name is self-explanatory, grew out of this ambience, though it utilized certain innovative techniques:

> Dick? Probably because it was the best-known slang word for detective, and therefore the most appropriate given name. Tracy? Probably because the super-sleuth was always tracing down his man.

> Dick Tracy was something brand-new in comics. He broke the rules, dared to flout taboos. "Back in 1931," says Gould, "no cartoon had ever shown a detective character fighting it out face to face with crooks via the hot lead route." Now in 1931, for the first time, comics actually showed murder, kid-

©1973 Chicago Tribune—New York News Syndicate.

Dick Tracy

napping, bloody fist fights, gory gunplay—"foul crime in detail," with all its shocking brutality.

According to Queen, there were two basic influences on Gould—the first, already mentioned, involved the seeming breakdown of society and the development of near-anarchic conditions. In such a situation Tracy stands as a symbol of goodness, "that absolutely honest and incorruptible defender of the faith with his Rock of Gibraltar sense of duty . . . with not a soft line in his character or appearance . . . or the way he pounced, pummeled, pursued . . . or the way *he* examined the scene of a crime . . . that true-blue, indomitable, granite-featured figure and his vigorous, slangy, crisply emphatic speech . . . that iron-willed man who, ahead of his time, was never uptight, who never blew his cool."

His stance is particularly important because if he cannot destroy crime, whenever it comes to his attention, the whole moral fiber of American culture becomes threatened. Thus his acts have implications far beyond the seeming triviality of many of his cases.

The second major influence on Gould, according to Queen, was the development of the action-detective story in the twenties. (Perhaps the naturalism of the period itself influenced the action-detective novel.) Queen argues quite conclusively that Dick Tracy was "the world's first procedural detective of fiction, in the modern sense. And the discovery is even more startling when we realize that the world's first procedural detective made his debut not in prose but in pictures, that he entered the mainstream of the mystery genre not in a book or magazine but in a newspaper."

Although Queen's essay is impressionistic, it does capture the essence of the strip and some of its significant cultural and psychological aspects. The ambience of morbidity and passion that pervades the strip reflects its Calvinistic underpinnings. The various grotesques who populate the strip, making it a veritable bestiary of criminal monstrosities, are graphically represented demons whose physical ugliness shows their moral ugliness. As Wolfgang Kayser put it in his study of the grotesque, it is *"an attempt to invoke and subdue the demonic aspects of the world."* On a graphic level, then, Gould's use of grotesque figures is quite significant—apart from the story line.

The grotesque describes someone (or something) fantastically ugly—such as a human being that is part animal. Gould's menagerie involves such creatures as The Mole (and now his daughter Molene), Rhodent, and Piggy. But even his villains who are not animal-like are incredibly ugly: Flattop, Shoulders, The Brow, Flyface, Spots, The Pouch, or Ugly Christine, to name only a few. In addition to having their physical ugliness show their moral ugliness, the grotesques facilitate an easy recognition of "good" and "evil" in general.

There is not much in the way of ambiguity or complexity in *Dick Tracy*. People are either good or bad and are identified as such. Naming a character after his particular vice is an old technique borrowed from morality plays. The use of grotesques, actually, is a characteristic of American literature, as well as popular culture. The late William Van

O'Connor, former chairman of the English Department of the University of California at Davis, makes this point in a book called *The Grotesque: An American Genre.* Many of our greatest writers, O'Connor suggests, have used grotesques—from our earliest writers to such modern giants as Faulkner and Anderson.

Anderson said that anyone who pursued a single truth until it warped his sense of truth and reality was a grotesque, and this is the feeling you get from looking at, as well as reading, *Dick Tracy.* The characters are all one-dimensional, and the frame of reference with which they all see the world is distorted. The passion and intensity mount until it becomes almost insupportable. The grim and brutal criminals become locked in mortal combat with a grim and relentless Tracy. A sense of terror slowly develops, as the ugly and sinister types proceed with their activities. The tension is finally released by the violence with which Tracy disposes of his opponents.

Gould was the first comic strip artist to use violence, as I have already pointed out. *The strip is permeated by a sense of violence that is imminent, even if there is not actually a great deal of violence in the strip* (in terms of frame counts showing violent actions). The criminals are violent and so is Tracy, except that his use of violence, because it is within the law, is portrayed as morally acceptable. There is something incongruous about the fact that Tracy, a super-technocratic police officer, generally has to resort to physical violence in apprehending the various criminals he battles. In spite of his wrist-radios and space coupés, he generally is obligated to punch the criminals in the nose or shoot them through the head. (In recent years, as a result of a great deal of concern about the possible harmful effects of violence in comics, Gould has toned down the strips, though his use of grotesques continues.)

Dick Tracy reflects the world as a sinful, corrupt, degrading place. This stems directly from our evangelical Protestant tradition. Tracy is our superego, developed almost to the point of pathology: he tells us there is no escape from judgment, even if you "seem" to be getting away with something. Thus he stems from a long line of conscience-ridden Protestants who have peopled this country and worked mightily to vanquish evil—in both thought and deed. This explains the rather oppressive ambience of the strip, for it reflects a pathological preoccupation with the evil and corruption that permeates the world. In such a world there must be eternal vigilance; attention must be paid to every manifestation of evil, no matter how seemingly trivial, for the power of evil to corrupt the good and to destroy man and his democratic institutions is a central tenet of this view.

The relentless pursuit of evildoers, the almost overpowering sense of guilt and fear of evil, and the inevitable triumph of the good and the destruction of the evil are very much a part of the working and lower-class evangelical Protestant tradition, tinged with remnants from Puritan thought. Curiously enough, the intensity I've been discussing is tied to the separation of church and state in America; in Europe, where sin was recognized as part of man and therefore fit into the scheme of things, there is no necessity for bloody avengers. As Stanley Elkins has written (in *Slavery*) about sin (in Europe):

> . . . an actual place had been made for it in life's crucial experience. It had been classified from time out of mind and given specific names; the reality of "lust," "avarice," and "oppression" had given rise to the most intricate of social arrangements, not for eliminating them, but for softening their impact and limiting their scope—for protecting the weak and defining the responsibilities of the strong . . .

> What, then, might be expected to happen if *sin* should suddenly become apparent, in a nation whose every individual was, at least, symbolically, expected to stand on his own two feet? The reaction was altogether destructive. The sense of outrage was personal, the sense of personal *guilt* was crushing. The gentle American of mild vices was transformed into the bloody avenger.

It is this sense of guilt and outrage that is at the root of many of our reformist movements, and which has sanctioned violence—since it is defined, then, as justifiable. Tracy can be seen as a symbol of this evangelical Protestant bitterness about an evil world, an avenger who will root out evil that is trying to intrude into a (potentially, at least) good society.

In addition to being an avenger, an instrument of the just, God-fearing and honest people, Tracy has another important function. He is the hero who undergoes *ordeals*. Ellery Queen paints a fascinating picture of some of these ordeals that Tracy suffers:

> Now join Dick Tracy in some of his danger-packed, breath-

taking, hair's-breadth adventures and escapes—Dick Tracy versus Organized Crime—Dick Tracy slugged, pistol-whipped, tortured, burned, beaten, pressurized, dynamited, dragged by a car at 60 miles an hour, stabbed, crushed (especially his shooting hand), victim of concussions, fractures (usually compound), cracked ribs, dislocated hip—in the course of 39 years of crime-busting, a veritable encyclopedia of harrowing experiences, "grisly business" "gruesome, sinister, fiendish havoc" (a combination of Chester Gould's own words), and impossible-to-get-out-of predicaments. . . .

As Queen points out, Tracy is indestructible, which is, of course, a requirement of the strip. One of the necessities of a comic strip from a structural point of view is that its hero must survive. But beyond this technicality, what is the significance of all these ordeals Tracy undergoes?

The ordeal is part of the general myth of the hero, a myth which seems to be ubiquitous, and which deals with the attempts of people (at whatever level of cultural development, it seems) to explain the human condition and man's place in the universe. The hero has an elevated status, but the cost of this superior position is the need to undergo "tests" and to suffer. Suffering ordeals purifies the hero and, at the same time, purifies society. The similarity between Tracy's ordeals and various initiative rituals of primitive societies is striking. Take, for example, Mircea Eliade's description of primitive initation rites in *The Sacred and the Profane*:

> . . . the ideal of humanity that the primitive wishes to attain he sets on a superhuman plane. This means: (1) one does not become a complete man until one has passed beyond,

and in some sense abolished, "natural" humanity, for initiation is reducible to a paradoxical, supernatural experience of death and resurrection or of second birth: (2) initiation rites, entailing ordeals and symbolic death and resurrection, were instituted by gods, culture heroes, or mythical ancestors; hence these rites have a superhuman origin, and by performing them the novice imitates a superhuman, divine action.

Tracy's ordeals (and the ordeals of military heroes, and various other modern heroic types) are rooted in the notion that man must be tested, symbolically killed, and then reborn, with a more profound knowledge of reality. The fight between the hero and the monster is a basic mythic motif, and Tracy is merely a modern instance of this theme, in a somewhat camouflaged format.

Tracy's ordeals may in some way represent a notion found in the evangelical Protestant view that life itself is an ordeal, in which we are always being tested by Satanic forces, always being tempted by evil figures. His ability to survive all ordeals, to keep to the straight and narrow path, serves us as a model of what is possible; it reassures us that we can avoid temptation and survive troubles. For Tracy demonstrates, over and over again, that good is stronger than evil, that God is stronger than the Devil. In one strip Tracy says (about criminals): "They can't win!" Of course! For in a fundamentalist Christian view of things, God and goodness always will triumph. All that is needed, ultimately, is faith.

The existence of criminals, Gould's grotesques, is in fact part of the scheme of things. They exist to test us and make possible our redemption, our development. As formal religious practice has declined (and statistics demonstrate this conclusively), a problem has presented itself. How do we rid ourselves of the sense of guilt which religion used to help assuage? This is now done for us by other means, one of which is the detective story or detective comic strip. The structure of the strip, with its victims, evildoers, and agents of God's wrath and divine justice, is all very formalized and very much like a ritual itself. It is repeated over and over again, though there are always certain variations of a minor nature.

The grotesques facilitate a kind of "guilt-free aggression" on the part of the readers. They are so repulsive and so easily identifiable that we can release our hostile antipathies against them with little feeling of remorse. This is an important function of all art forms; the term *catharsis* is well-known in literary criticism, though I think that what happens is more than just a release of tension.

Dr. George R. Bach and Peter Wyden explain the problem of aggression release in *The Intimate Enemy*:

> Change and aggression go together, and since change is essential to growth and survival, man has a surplus capacity for aggression and a high creativity for inventing new ways of directly and indirectly releasing it. Man is in a chronic state of aggression-overmobilization. Each individual has, therefore, an embarrassing stockpile of surplus aggression in readiness and he must do something constantly or periodically to release some of it. Consequently, man is in a constant search for enemies who can serve as safe aggression-release targets. All segments of a culture (not just politicians) share in the search for and/or invention of enemies; once found, people go after them with hostile gusto, as history amply demonstrates.

In this respect, one of the essential functions of *Dick Tracy* for the reader is to defuse him by providing acceptable targets for his aggressive feelings. Gould's genius lies in his ability to serve our needs with an endless procession of grotesques who, like all criminals, seem to cry out for containment, who purposively seem to sow the seeds of their own destruction.

At no time, of course, is anything ever said about the *society* that continually creates such monsters. We are led to believe that they are mutations of sorts, and when we are rid of them there will be law and order, or the good society.

Dick Tracy (as well as detective stories) may be a form of religious ritual of a desacralized nature, in a seemingly demythologized society. The elements which tie him to the sacred are present, but there is little overt identification with religion *per se*. Tracy's triumphs, aside from their spiritual significnce, also demonstrate the essential viability of the social system and the values which inform this social system. We can indulge in vicarious thrills under an "aesthetic illusion," and participate in activities that we fear, knowing all the time that it is just fantasy and that Tracy will triumph, no matter what! There is probably a certain element of boredom and escapism motivating us, also; but these matters are incidental to the essential function of the strip, which is to help us resolve our feelings of guilt by providing scapegoats. The grotesques simplify things for us greatly.

In some way they may even represent the evil side of our own nature, which we can recognize and then deal with. A number of critics have suggested that readers of detective mysteries identify with *both* the detective and the murderer, who represent the good and evil sides of their nature. This would suggest that adventure stories provide a place where our internal conflicts can be worked out. Perhaps it is even similar to battles between our superegos (conscience) and ids (desires). In this respect, reading *Dick Tracy* may allow us to work through some of our own personal problems, to test ourselves, and to effect a resolution on the side of goodness or socially approved behavior. The grotesques are so foul and so monstrous that the battle we have to fight is an easy one, for we cannot allow that side of our nature to triumph; it is too unappealing. Besides, as Tracy continually demonstrates, criminals come to bad ends—though a few do reform in the strip.

The gangster is a familiar figure in contemporary popular culture—in part because of Gould's fecund imagination. The gangster is a more modern manifestation of the robber or rustler of cowboy days. Just as the sheriff, representative of an agrarian society, has given way to the detective, so has the rustler given way to the gangster. The latter two figures, the detective and the gangster, are essentially urbanized figures who function in an industrialized, mechanized setting.

Some sociologists believe, as I have already mentioned, that the gangster is particularly American, a character whose need for success overwhelms his conscience and allows him to function outside the law. As Daniel Bell says (quoted in S.M. Lipset, *First New Nation*):

Crime, in many ways, is a Coney Island mirror caricaturing

the morals and manners of a society. The jungle quality of the American business community particularly at the turn of the century, was reflected in the mode of "business" practiced by the coarse gangster elements, most of them from new immigrant families, who were "getting ahead," just as Horatio Alger had urged. . . .

The desires satisfied in extra-legal fashion were more than a hunger for the "forbidden fruits" of conventional morality. They also involved the complex and ever shifting structure of group, class and ethnic stratification, which is the warp and woof of America's "open" society, such "normal" goals as independence through a business of one's own, and such "moral" aspirations as the desire for social advancement and social prestige. For crime, in the language of the sociologists, has a "functional" role in the society, and the urban rackets —the illicit activity organized for continuing profit, rather than individual illegal acts— . . . [are] one of the queer ladders of social mobility in American life.

Crime is functional in that it facilitates social mobility, which is the essence of the American Dream, and which helps preserve political stability. Crime, then, is both functional (for the individuals rising in the world, if they succeed as criminals, and the society which is stabilized by their social mobility) *and* dysfunctional, in that the legal system is being attacked and the social fabric rent.

There is a particular quality to the success-drive of the gangster (the most significant kind of criminal), and that is some kind of a *subconscious suicidal intent*. Robert Warshaw sees the gangster as a tragic hero, finding him tragic because he must struggle against overwhelming odds (the need to keep expanding his territory; his conflicts with other gangsters, as well as the law), which leads inevitably to his violent death.

In a fascinating study, *Suicide and Scandinavia,* Herbert Hendin lists seven patterns which explain the psychodynamics of suicide:

> . . . death as abandonment, death as omnipotent mastery, death as retroflexed murder, death as a reunion, death as rebirth, death as self-punishment or atonement, and death as a phenomenon that in an emotional sense has already taken place.

The gangster is probably best characterized by a sense of "omnipotent mastery through death," which Hendin says gives "a person an illusory feeling of mastery over a situation through the control of life and death." There is a certain amount of atonement involved in his death also. He pays his debt to society with his life.

The gangster is a hero in the sense that he is a transcendental figure, a person who risks his life, who asserts himself in the face of society. He pays with his life for his transgressions, but he has also, generally speaking, taken life. *He plays God but is only a mortal and is thus doomed.* This is the way he is frequently portrayed, though the gangster is becoming an increasingly outmoded figure. For one thing he is being replaced in popular culture by the secret agent, a character who roams the world and kills legally. He murders in the national interest, and this is seen as justifiable. Second, the contemporary gangster tends to be part of a large business-like organization which is rationalized just like legal corporations, and in which there is much less thrill. As this has happened, or to the degree that this has happened, the gangster has lost his appeal and fascination.

In a sense, then, *Dick Tracy* is an old-fashioned strip which reflects a society that has rapidly grown away from him. The strip among other functions, allows us to attain a guilt-free release of our aggressions. It might be logical to expect that the secret agent will replace the detective, but I do not think that will be the case—for the detective and his relation to crime and evil are rooted in the evangelical Protestant tradition and related to American values which seem, still, to be meaningful to large numbers of people. James Bond has come and gone (besides, he is an English figure and the spy story is essentially an English invention); and Tracy has continued on in his relentless pursuit of crime, a servant of a stern God, in a never-ending quest for the sublimity of a community of saints.

FLASH GORDON
The Triumph of the Democratic Will

Flash Gordon made its dramatic advent on the Sunday page of January 7, 1934. The first panel shows part of a newspaper whose headline reads "World Coming to an End —Strange New Planet Rushing Toward Earth—Only Miracle Can Save Us, Says Science." This single panel is filled with interesting possibilities. First, a calamity may cause the end of the world, suggesting the strip has something of an eschatological nature. Concern with the end of the world is not new in mankind, and the possibility of the world coming to an end, through collision with other planets, is a staple of science fantasy.

Implicit in the notion of the cataclysmic end of the

133

world is the matter of divine retribution; mythically as well as in religion, man will be punished for his transgressions on Judgment Day. The question arises concerning whether the world will actually be destroyed or not; a Supreme Deity may just be warning man, and a miraculous redemption is always conceivable. The fact that it is an *unknown* planet that is hurtling toward earth serves to emphasize man's pettiness and powerlessness. He may have science but, as the headline tells us, the existence of a strange new planet shows that science is not as powerful a tool as we might think. "There are more things in heaven and earth" than we think, as the new planet demonstrates.

The next three panels show the impact of the impending calamity on different peoples. In Africa, the natives beat tom-toms and "the howling blacks await their doom." In the desert, "the Arab . . . resigned to the inevitable, faces Mecca and prays for his salvation." We see a picture of an Arab, his arms outstretched, praying underneath a sky streaked with red. And in Times Square in New York, "a seething mass of humanity watches a bulletin board describe the flight of the comet." Mankind is paralyzed, and waiting for the inevitable.

Except, that is, for one Dr. Hans Zarkov, a scientist who works day and night to perfect a device to save the world. His brain weakens under the strain, and when Flash Gordon and Dale Arden parachute down to his laboratory, Zarkov forces them to join him in his rocket, which he hopes can deflect the comet from its course. Flash Gordon, Yale man and polo player, was a passenger in a plane whose wing was wrecked by a meteor. He grabbed Dale Arden, the only other passenger, in his arms and parachuted to earth, landing by chance in Zarkov's grounds near his laboratory. The last two panels show Zarkov's rocket blasting off. The captions read, "With a deafening roar, Dr. Zarkov's rocket ship, with Flash and Dale aboard, shrieks into the heavens —and heads straight toward the onrushing planet with a madman at the controls!"

Eventually they discover that the planet is on an eccentric orbit and will not crash into the earth; they land on the strange planet and have all kinds of wondrous adventure. The three form a team; Flash Gordon (another comic-strip upper-class aristocrat) has great strength and courage; Zarkov has technological genius; and Dale Arden, whose name suggests nature and loyalty, provides a love interest.

Although *Flash Gordon,* which was created to compete with *Buck Rogers,* is essentially a science fiction epic, there is also a great deal of attention paid to romance in the strip. Love motivates many of the characters, and Flash Gordon often finds himself in delicate situations because women are always falling in love with him. Alex Raymond, who wrote and drew the strip, had a style very much influenced by fashion illustrators. He was an excellent draftsman and delighted in carefully drawn pictures of women in various revealing costumes and states of seminudity. Considering the times, Raymond's women were very sexy, with well-developed breasts, and slim legs. He lavished a great deal of attention on the drawing of breasts, which were usually detailed with lines and shadows.

Although romance plays a large role, *Flash Gordon* is basically a story dealing with the heroic exploits of a bold adventurer, who brings freedom and democracy to alien worlds, fights injustice and tyranny, and destroys all kinds of hideous monsters and brutal despots along the way. Science fiction, like utopian novels, essentially deals with social and political considerations, and it is man as a social and political animal that is its basic subject.

Dick Allen, editor of *Science Fiction: The Future,* explains science fiction as follows:

> . . . a mainstay of SF stories is the situation in which humans are locked on a spaceship bound for another galaxy; they must devise their own society and formulate its rules. In an alternative version, they have landed on an alien planet and must organize a new world structure.

This is exactly what happens in *Flash Gordon;* when they land on the planet, they find a brutal totalitarian regime controlling most of the planet, which they ultimately destroy.

One of the reasons science fiction is so popular, Allen suggests, is that science fiction writers are

> able to deal cogently with this increasingly incomprehensible world; and they generally do this without bundling their characters up in tight little knots of despair. Science fiction has always been a popular form of epic and romantic literature; its heroes are larger than life; its plots deal with the fate of entire societies; its basic motivations are those of quest and self-discovery; its affirmation is that of the power of the human to adjust to fate. In science fiction, man, the individual man, still makes a difference. The hero may be part of a vast cooperative organization but he finds, like James Bond,

ways of expressing his individuality within that organization, generally without feeling a need to either overthrow or escape the organization. The SF hero, in other words, is no anti-hero doomed from the start.

Flash Gordon, then, has the appeals of the science fiction story as well as those of the well-drawn comic strip. Raymond's capacity to create hideous monsters and ugly villains (as well as lovely heroines), and his affirmation of man's possibilities, struck an agreeable chord with the American people.

To be sure, the strip relied on clichés, as most comic strips do. The language is purple and overly dramatic, the figures tend to be uni-dimensional, and Raymond's use of science might be rather simple-minded. But the notion that the individual does make a difference, despite everything, as well as Flash Gordon's mission—spreading democracy— are parts of the American ethos, and the strip is, in this sense, a truly American document. The notion of the omni-competent individual and the sense of mission are fundamental in the American mind, according to R.H. Gabriel, and the leap into outer space may have been necessitated by a belief that this was a new frontier for us. We had already fought, and won, a war which was to make the world safe for democracy.

The frontier, so to speak, was settled; we needed new vistas and outer space provided them. The thirties was a period of considerable interest in science fiction. It was "the Gernsback era," according to Isaac Asimov, when *Amazing Stories* was flourishing, along with several other competi-

MINGO IS A CITY OF FIESTA AND CARNIVAL, MADLY CHEERING "*FLASH AND FREEDOM!*" IN WILD JOY OVER THE END OF MING'S CRUEL REIGN.

1.

FLASH, ZARKOV AND ERGON WORK TIRE-
LESSLY IN SOLVING THE MANY PROBLEMS
OF FOUNDING A FREE, JUST AND SAFE
GOVERNMENT—"WE'RE READY FOR
BARIN," SAYS FLASH. "I'LL SEND FOR
HIM IN THE MORNING. IT WILL
BE UP TO YOU, ERGON, TO
SEE THAT MING IS WELL
GUARDED."

2

AT SUNRISE, A FAST
PURSUIT ROCKET ROARS
OUT OF MINGO AND POINTS
TOWARD ARBORIA,
DISTANT HOME OF
PRINCE BARIN, THE
RIGHTFUL HEIR TO
THE THRONE OF
MONGO.

3

MEANWHILE, MING'S AMAZING BRAIN HAS SECRETLY FOUGHT OFF THE EFFECTS OF ZARKOV'S HYPNO-SERUM. BY PRETENDING A DEEP, DRUGGED SLEEP, HE LULLS THE WATCHFULNESS OF HIS GUARD—

6-25-41.

4

SUDDENLY, DISASTER THREATENS FLASH'S NEW NATION OF FREEDOM! ERGON DISCOVERS THE TRAGEDY-- THE MURDER OF HIS CARELESS GUARD AND THE TYRANT'S ESCAPE!

NEXT WEEK: IN THE TYRANT'S POWER ~

5.

tors. And it was the period when *Buck Rogers* and *Flash Gordon* were launched.

There is probably an element of escapism behind the popularity of science fiction in the period. We were in the middle of a depression which negated our sense of possibility and put dampers on our hopes. We needed to get away from the cares of the world, and did it by leaving the world behind, literally as well as figuratively. But we could not leave behind our belief systems and values, and though Flash Gordon may explore new worlds, he brings with him his traditional American point of view. He is a futuristic pioneer, but a pioneer nevertheless, out to tame the wilderness and spread Americanism to the outer edges of the universe.

The frontier had, many historians believe, a special place in our history. According to Turner, who first elaborated the "frontier theory," the fact that Americans had vast expanses of virgin forest, that we had "nature" so to speak, led to the development of the American character (bold, innovative, practical, equalitarian) and to uniquely American institutions. It allowed men to escape from traditions and historical institutions and create themselves anew. Having an abundance of nature made it possible for will power to be efficacious; there was opportunity for all. The only question, ultimately, was that of will.

It is this notion, that will power is important, that is central to *Flash Gordon*. Again and again he launches himself into adventures and combats that seem hopeless, only to emerge triumphant. *Flash Gordon* is actually a study in the triumph of the democratic will. The very first adventure in the collection of *Flash Gordon* published by the Nostalgia Press starts in a forest, where the only free people on the planet of Mongo live. It is nestled in vast trees and called Arberia.

Mongo is ruled by a murderous dictator, Ming the Merciless. He has banished his daughter, Aura, and her husband, Prince Barin, to the forest and deprived them of modern arms. It is like something from Robin Hood—foresters armed with bows and arrows, living in nature. These good people stand in dramatic contrast to the inhabitants of Mingo, the central city of the planet. There Ming and his cohorts rule over a debased and enslaved populace, all of whom have shaved heads by order of Ming (who is bald).

If Ming represents one kind of cruelty, that of the civilized despot with an arsenal of esoteric machines of war at his command, there is another kind of ruler also to be destroyed. That is the barbarian, personified by a gigantic brute named Brukka, who inhabits vast caves and leads a band of evil, hairy giants. What we have here is a classic polarity in the American mind—especially the American mind of the nineteenth century. To the nineteenth-century American, nature represented some kind of a middle ground between the extremes of civilization (decadence) and barbarism (brutality). According to John William Ward, the American of the Jacksonian period wanted to avoid the extremes of "the savagery of unqualified nature and the degeneracy of overdeveloped civilization."

In this scheme of things nature represented a break with European civilization and its corrupting influences—

nature made democracy possible. Free from the chains of the past, man could lead the good life. These notions lasted well into the twentieth-century, and even today there are many Americans who believe that will power and beneficent nature are all that is needed to create the good society. In this view, democracy becomes that which facilitates will power; the state is viewed in negative terms and society is seen as an abstraction—a name for a collection of strong-willed individuals, each pursuing his own interest, and the interest of each leads, somehow, to the welfare or well-being of all.

The collection ends with the overthrowing of the despot, Ming. Flash Gordon, his friends and allies stage a revolt which topples Ming from power and leads to the development of a republic. Some of the captions in the strip are most instructive. After defeating Ming, Flash Gordon makes an announcement over the spacephone network: "This nation is now the republic of Mongo, founded on the principles of freedom and justice for all." Mongo becomes "The United Republics of Mongo," and it is led by a president elected by the people. But at this moment, Zarkov establishes radio contact with earth and finds that a new world war is breaking out. Gordon asks Zarkov to build a rocket so they can return to earth, but Dale Arden objects, saying she's had her fill of fighting.

Flash Gordon replies, good democrat that he is,

Peace? Happiness? How could we rest knowing that we have in our hands the knowledge, formulas and weapons to save our earth from the scourge that threatens to consume it? There will be no peace for me until all men are free!

Dale replies, "Yes . . . you're right, Flash. I'm ashamed of my selfishness. Your cause is mine—always will be." The book ends with Flash Gordon departing from Mongo, in a rocket equipped with the "most advanced war weapons of the planet."

The adventure described above ended in June of 1941, a short period before America became involved in World War II. Hitler had invaded Russia in June, and it seemed unlikely that Russia would hold. The world was teetering on the edge of another war, and the American mind was trying to justify American involvement in this war. Flash Gordon's speech about the impossibility of peace until all are free represents, I think, the kind of thinking that most Americans were doing. We saw our self-interest as dictating a free world; we would be threatened, ultimately, if *any* totalitarian regime existed.

The notion that the freedom of each is dependent on the freedom of all is one which has been very important in American history. It has formed our foreign policy, though it is probably also correct to say that the missionary ideal has been a kind of front for our predatory foreign trade practices. But as a model the notion is most significant. What is curious about this is that the interdependence model which we apply to foreign relations contrasts strongly with our individualistic ethos. Probably our assertiveness as individuals becomes transposed to the nation-state, so that we find ourselves in the curious position of seeing ourselves as independent individuals, with no society to speak of, and also as a great nation-state.

Ultimately *Flash Gordon* reassures us that the heroic

individual, with will power and intelligence (science) will triumph over all adversaries, and that his triumph and the triumphs of millions like him insure the ultimate triumph of freedom and democracy. The relationship that exists between will power and the fates is never adequately resolved; this is a problem we inherited from our Puritan fathers. But there is little doubt that morality and goodness, when allied with determination, cannot be denied. This is shown in repeated episodes in the strip in which Flash Gordon is seemingly killed. Inevitably, of course, he is brought back to life and succeeds in defeating his adversaries. If, in the final analysis, all encounters and battles are contingent upon will power, we can rest assured. *Flash Gordon* demonstrates over and over again that goodness is more powerful than evil and that history is the record of the triumph of the democratic will.

DISSOCIATION IN A HERO
Superman and the Divided Self

Even Superman is in for a change. In future issues he will come to feel that he is a stranger in an imperfect world, the editors say. Surveying ant-like hordes of human beings from a skyscraper, he muses in one forthcoming issue, "For the first time in many years, I feel that I'm alone."

"Superman was created in the Depression as an icon, a Nietzsche superman," says Carmine Infantino, National's editorial director. "At that time, people needed a perfect being. But now they want someone they can relate to. Like kids today, the new Superman will suffer from an inability to belong."
—RICHARD J. HOWE, *The Wall Street Journal*, April 15, 1970

Comic-book cultists are fascinated by how the superheroes were born and developed. The saga of how Superman traveled from the doomed planet Krypton to Earth aboard a rocket and was discovered by kindly old Jonathan and Martha Kent is, of course, as familiar to cultists as the

146

legend of Washington and the cherry tree.

They also know the original Superman did not possess X-ray vision or superhearing, and that his ineffectual alter-image pitched a fumbling pass at Lois Lane on page 11 of the summer 1939 issue of Superman's magazine (He: "Why is it you always avoid me at the office? She [looking away] "Please Clark! I've been scribbling sob stories all day long. Don't ask me to dish out another"). The cool, unapproachable Miss Lane, of course, was hung up on Clark Kent's hidden self—the indigo-haired Man of Steel—right from the first issue (She: "But when will I see you again?" He [looking away]: "Who knows? Perhaps tomorrow—perhaps never").

—*Newsweek,* February 15, 1965 (p. 89)

In recent years Superman has been changing. As Jules Feiffer described it in "Pop Sociology," (*New York Herald Tribune,* January 9, 1966) the changes have been quite significant:

> In my day Superman was the total individualist, unfettered by either the laws of gravity or the courts of justice. Today's Superman has, like the rest of us, *responsibilities.* He has two emasculating girl reporters competing with each other to see whose life he has to save more often. He has a hero-worshiping cub reporter he has to look after. He even has Batman and Robin (and a host of other masked, caped and leotarded heroes) suddenly dropping in on short visits from rival comic books, expecting to be looked after, expecting to be taken care of. So, married or not, Superman's a family man, loaded with other people's demands, other people's problems. Is it any wonder that these days he often has his weaknesses, his failures—that, in a recent issue, he lost a fight to a *girl*? One difference between our idealism in the thirties and our cynicism in the sixties is that, today, we even allow our Supermen to turn impotent.

When we discarded our old legacy of rugged individualism

and self-sufficiency, we also abandoned the view that a heroic super-powerful individual might solve all our problems with some magnificent gesture.

But what is important about Superman is not that he is changing; most of the comic book superheroes are becoming more "relevant" and are involved with social problems such as racism and war and reflect various psychological difficulties. It is what Superman represents, as a symbol, *before* he started changing that I am most interested in; and it is his symbolic significance that is most important, I feel, for our purposes.

Though he may have been a relatively simple-minded hero in the old days before he became socially conscious, *as a symbolic figure he presents many difficulties.* This is because his symbolic significance has many different dimensions. For example, the notion of a superman, a strong, heroic figure who transcends ordinary man, has obvious Oedipal interpretations. The desire of young boys to rid themselves of their fathers coupled with their need for the knowledge and protection of their fathers is very closely realized in the role Superman plays in his adventures.

Superman also is a superego figure, a symbol of conscience. He is pledged to be a champion of the oppressed and to help people in need. In the course of his activities he often must fight with evil, and his triumphs can be seen, from a Freudian perspective, as representing the dominance of a highly developed superego. (The superego is defined as "a major sector of the psyche that is only partly conscious and that aids in character formation by reflecting parental conscience and the rules of society" *Webster's Seventh Col-*

legiate). Good-guy superheroes have this function, no doubt, but Superman's fantastic powers make the superego's dominance most apparent. Dick Tracy, a rather morbid and perhaps pathological figure, also represents a highly developed superego, but he is, at least, human and vulnerable. Superman, possessing all kinds of super-powers, cannot be denied!

The very fact that Superman has such prodigious powers presents a problem to his writers. They are forced to create various extraordinary challenges for Superman, so there can be some question about the resolution of the various adventures. In some ways he must be humanized, so that he does not merely wipe out his antagonists. Kryptonite, the fragments of the planet where Superman was born before he was sent to earth, thus make it conceivable that he will be foiled, though all comic book readers know that their heroes will ultimately triumph.

The use of a substance that makes superior aliens vulnerable is common in science fiction and can be found in H.G. Wells's *The War of the Worlds*. In that story, harmless germs kill the superior aliens from Mars (who represent a certain type of villain, the bug-eyed monsters). These monsters, with "minds that are to our minds as ours are to those of the beasts that perish" are similar in power to Superman, except that he is good and identifies with mankind. The question that Wells brings up is: how do we (earthlings) relate to superior and hostile aliens? How do we deal with them? The answer he offers in his particular story is not hopeful. However, by using the device of the weakening or destructive substance he is able to resolve the dilem-

Superman
© 1973 National Periodical Publications, Inc.

ma and find a way for mankind to survive in the face of powers beyond comprehension.

We have, to this point, been discussing Superman from a psychological standpoint—as a figure representing the superego who must, somehow, be diminished and humanized so there can be suspense and a question about how his adventures will be resolved. But he may also be analyzed from a sociological and political standpoint. After all, there is something strange about a democratic, equalitarian society having a hero who represents values that are antithetical to our basic beliefs, and which have been associated with Nazi Germany, in particular, and European elitist culture in general.

There is a fairly close relationship, generally, between a society and its heroes; if a hero does not espouse values that are meaningful to his readers, there seems little likelihood that he will be popular. The term "super" means over, above, higher in quantity, quality or degree, all of which conflict with the American equalitarian ethos. I believe the answer to this dilemma lies in Superman's qualities and character. He is, despite his awesome powers, rather ordinary—so much so that he poses as a spectacled nonentity of a reporter in order to avoid publicity and maintain some kind of privacy.

His superiority lies in his powers, and though he possesses great physical attributes and abilities, they are always at the service of his fellow man. He is not, by any means, an aristocrat who values "breeding" and has a sense of superiority. An everyman with superhuman capacities, what Emerson said about Napoleon can also be said of

Superman; he is "the idol of the common men because he had in transcendent degree the qualities and powers of common men" ("Napoleon, Man of the World").

Thus a difference in degree (of power) has not led to a difference in kind (sense of superiority). It might even be said that Superman is rather shy and quite bland. In a society which will not tolerate pretensions, which has no hereditary aristocracy, even Superman is forced to present himself as a supreme democrat. He is an ordinary person who just happens to be the strongest man in the world. *Webster's Seventh Collegiate* defines a superman as "a superior man that according to Nietzsche has learned to forgo fleeting pleasures and attain happiness and dominance through the exercise of creative power." This is very close to the basic middle-class American pattern of deferred gratification—you give up minor pleasures of the moment for better pleasures later. In many respects Superman is a middle-class square!

The problem that Superman faces is that, as a superior man in a society which is stridently equalitarian, he must disguise himself, lest people be envious and cause difficulties. In the tale of his origin this is made evident. A scientist from the doomed planet Krypton sends his infant child to earth, where it is discovered by an elderly couple, the Kents. They place him in an orphanage and later adopt him. In the fifth frame of the origin tale (which takes only two pages), Mr. Kent says to young Clark: "Now listen to me, Clark! This great strength of yours—you've got to hide it from people or they'll be scared of you!"

And Mrs. Kent adds: "But when the proper time

comes, you must use it to assist humanity."

As he grows older, his powers develop. After his foster-parents die, we find the following:

> Clark decided he must turn his titanic strength into channels that would benefit mankind. And so was created—Super-man, champion of the oppressed, the physical marvel who had sworn to devote his existence to helping those in need.

The language almost has a Biblical ring, with the use of the passive tense in "and so was created." This suggests that his origin has a mythical dimension, and perhaps a sacred one. The Biblical parallel is furthered by the similarity between the way Moses and Superman were found.

Superman is different from many other comic book superheroes in that his true identity is Superman and Clark Kent is a disguise. When dangerous situations develop, Kent strips off his clothes and leaps into action as Super-man, a caped crusader in a brilliant red and blue costume.

The matter of *identity* is one of the central problems of Superman. Underneath the mask, the persona of an incompetent reporter, is a Superman. There is some kind of schizoid split in having one person with two separate beings. As Kent, Superman is often fooled by Lois Lane; it is quite inconveivable that Superman would fall for her tricks, yet Superman and Clark Kent are the same person. It is almost as if there were two separate beings with complete dominance within their particular sphere of operations. When Superman is pretending to be Clark Kent, he actually is Clark Kent and when Superman is Superman, he bears no relation to Clark Kent, though they are one and the same being. Superman seems to be a "divided self," to use R.D. Laing's term from *The Divided Self*, except that Superman/Clark Kent does not seem to be psychotic.

There is a great deal of confusion in *Superman*. Clark Kent likes Lois Lane, who spurns him, while Lois Lane likes Superman, who in turn spurns her. We find ourselves in a situation in which a woman likes and dislikes the same man, or, rather his different identities. The only way we can explain such matters is to postulate two separate identities in the same person which are autonomous in their own particular realm.

In this respect the costumes Superman and all superheroes wear are significant. When he has his usual work suit on, and his glasses, Superman is not really Superman, so to speak. He is timid, somewhat incompetent, and terribly boring. It is only when he strips off his veneer and his suit, and emerges resplendent in his cape and leotards, that he acts like Superman. The Superclothes make the Superman; no doubt about that.

In *The Waning of the Middle Ages*, Huizinga explains the significance of clothes and costumes:

> The modern male costume since the end of the eighteenth century is essentially a workman's dress. Since political progress and social perfection have stood foremost in general appreciation, and the ideal itself is sought in the highest production and most equitable distribution of goods, there is no longer any need for playing the hero or the sage. The ideal itself has become democratic. In aristocratic periods, on the

other hand, to be representative of true culture means to produce by conduct, by customs, by manners, by costume, by deportment, the illusion of a heroic being. . . .

But all the aristocratic aspects of the heroic being have been lost in an equalitarian society, so only the costume remains. It is the costume that counts, and Superman's costume is probably a version of the old costume of the swordsman and nobleman, brought up to date for pseudo science fiction.

Superman's lack of interest in Lois Lane correlates closely with symptoms found in schizophrenics. As Robert Waelder says in *Basic Theory of Psychoanalysis:*

> Two characteristic features of these patients—the difficulty of establishing contact with them, i.e., a deficiency in their object relations, and the fact that some, though not all of them, produce megalomanic ideas—seemed to be accountable by one single assumption, viz., that the libido had been withdrawn from the objects and concentrated upon the ego.

Waelder brings up this subject in his discussion of *narcissism*. The narcissist takes himself as an object of love, though it must be pointed out that self-love cannot be equated with self-interest; indeed, the two are often opposed to one another. The point is that a withdrawal of the libido and an element of self-love might possibly explain Superman's lack of interest in Lois Lane. As a Superman he has learned, so Nietzsche explains, to forgo fleeting pleasures—one of which may be romantic involvement with

Lois Lane, members of the opposite sex in general, and perhaps everyone. After all, a Superman "deserves" a Superwoman.

In a number of ways Superman's divided self and history are significant (and perhaps even paradigmatic) for American society and culture in general. Superman has left a destructive—in this case self-destructive—place of origin for a new world where his powers make him the strongest man on earth. His history is similar to that of the Puritans, who left a corrupt old world for a blissful new one, where their spiritual powers might flower. And like Superman the Puritans labored heroically for goodness and justice, as they interpreted both.

Just as Kryptonite weakens Superman so does contact with the corrupting old world weaken innocent Americans and destroy their moral integrity. Thomas Jefferson believed this to be the case, and the notion of America as innocent and Europe as corrupt is part of the conventional wisdom and mythology of the American mind. Superman, like the American, thus must avoid contact with the past in order to maintain his powers. With the American this has led to an antihistorical attitude, a belief in the future and repudiation of the past. We may have half the historians in the world teaching in our universities, but the basic frame of reference of the America mind is antihistorical.

We believe that when we left Europe and our fatherland, says Geoffrey Gorer in *The American People,* we escaped from time. We left institutions (such as the Roman Catholic Church, nobility, royalty), which are associated with history and escaped to the forest, where we became nature's noblemen. This nineteenth-century view of things still colors our beliefs; Americans tend to see themselves as simple people living in an arcadia. Rather than accept the fact that we live in an urbanized, bureaucratized, and industrialized society we take recourse in myths such as the notion of the self-made man who, if he has adequate will power, can realize any and all goals he sets for himself.

In this sense we all see ourselves as supermen. Beneath the facade of the bumbling, inefficient, or even rather ordinary white-collar worker is the superman, just waiting for his chance. Unfortunately, by the time the average man reaches his middle thirties, life seems to close in on him and he begins to realize that not much is likely to change, that he isn't a superman, and that heroic will power is not enough to help him realize his dreams. The tragedy is that our culture promotes fantastic expectations, which are rarely realized. Failure becomes all the more bitter. Since people have no one to blame except themselves; if success is personal and individual (being essentially a function of the super will), then so is failure.

The schizoid split within Superman symbolizes a basic split within the American psyche. Americans are split like Superman, alienated from their selves and bitter about the disparity between their dreams and their achievements, between the theory that they are in control of their own lives and the reality of their powerless and weakness.

Superman's identity problem is very similar to ours. The American's obsession with identity is a well-known phenomenon. It is because we have no sense of the past that we have no sense of who we are. Like Superman we perform superheroic tasks, one after the other, but they do not seem to give us any sense of being. Just as Superman keeps his identity hidden so do we hide ours by repudiating the past. And various Americanizing institutions, such as the schools, have prided themselves upon their ability to erase the ethnic identities of our immigrants and turn them into quintessential Americans within a generation or so. But we took their identities away with their traditions and practices and gave them nothing in return except a few myths and pipe dreams.

Originally Superman represented a heroic force who could use his super powers to lessen the impact of natural disasters or take direct action against criminals. As Marshall McLuhan puts it *The Mechanical Bride*:

> The attitudes of Superman to current social problems likewise reflect the strong-arm totalitarian methods the immature and barbaric mind. Like Daddy Warbucks in "Orphan Annie," Superman is ruthlessly efficient in carrying on a one-man crusade against crooks and anti-social forces. In neither case is their any appeal to the process of law. Justice is represented as an affair of personal strength alone. Any appraisal of the political tendencies of "Superman" (and also its many relatives in the comic-book world of violent adventure known as the "Squinky" division of entertainment) would have to include an admission that today the dreams of youths and adults alike seem to embody a mounting impatience with the laborious processes of civilized life and a restless eagerness to embrace violent solutions.

Superman, as an individualist, could not be expected to bother with red tape and delays and all the judicial processes which exist. Better a super bash in the teeth, which is quick and also allows readers to assuage their desire for vengeance and relieve themselves of aggressive feelings.

What has happened, ironically, is that instead of America becoming a society full of individual supermen (and the various manifestations of this concept such as the rugged individualist, the self-made man, the tycoon, etc.) just the opposite has occurred. The nineteenth-century notion postulated no society itself, so to speak; just a collection of supermen who happen to live in the same territory. Instead, what has happened is that America seems to be a society full of powerless weaklings, while the state has taken on the super-powers. We have a super-state with prodigious powers, while as individuals we feel feeble and unable to control our own destinies.

In the *Superman* comics, Krypton was introduced to facilitate plots but also for another reason, which is not apparent. We have a fear of power that is out of control, and Kryptonite helps us to relieve the anxiety caused by the presence of a power that cannot be controlled. But in present-day America there seems to be no moral equivalent of Kryptonite, to curb the powers of a super-state that seems to be out of control.

BATMAN AND THE
ARCHAIC EGO

The Aristocrat as Reformer

It is useful to look closely at the origin tale for *Batman*. Like *Superman's* origin tale it takes but two pages to compress a lifetime before the emergence of the hero. The first page of the origin tale is dominated by a massive figure of Batman in costume and the title "The Legend of the Batman—Who he is and how he came to be!" The story involves the brutal murder by a stick-up man of Thomas Wayne and his wife as they were returning one night, with Bruce, from a movie. As the caption reads in the panel which shows the dead parents, "the boy's eyes are wide with terror and shock as the horrible scene is spread before him." He says, "Father . . . Mother! . . . Dead! They're d . . . dead."

The scene shifts now to young Bruce kneeling at his bedside. The caption says, "Days later a curious and strange scene takes place." We see young Bruce kneeling in prayer, with his hands clasped. He says, "And I swear by the spirits of my parents to avenge their deaths by spending the rest of my life warring on all criminals." It is a sacred vow, similar to ones made by knights in medieval days, and suggests that there is a sacred dimension to his activities.

There is, in fact, a medieval quality to Batman's adventures. He himself is a figure closely related to shadow and mystery; the bat is a symbol of something deadly and strange, a nocturnal beast associated with vampirism and the occult. And Batman's nemesis, the Joker, also has a markedly sinister and symbolic dimension. The young boy makes his vow—to avenge the death of his parents by fighting all evil. However, he is doing more than fighting; he uses the phrase, "warring on all criminals," to give his exploits more emphasis. Batman is locked in a holy war— against evil in all its manifestations. His motivations are not generous at all. It is *vengeance,* a matter of getting even somehow, that is his justification. He is, like Superman and Little Orphan Annie, an *orphan* and as such is free to pursue his destiny without any complications.

He dedicates his life to his career and becomes a master scientist and superb athlete. He is also, we learn near the end of the origin tale, wealthy. We see him seated in what is obviously a mansion speculating to himself:

Dad's estate left me wealthy. I am ready . . . But first I must have a disguise. Criminals are a superstitious cowardly lot, so my disguise must be able to strike terror into their hearts. I must be a creature of the night. Black, terrible . . . A . . . A. . . .

As he sits, in a purple robe with yellow lapels, a huge bat flies in the open window. Wayne exclaims, "A bat! That's it! It's an omen. I shall become a *BAT*!" In the final frame of the origin tale we see a caped crusader, perched on a rooftop, under a full moon with bats gliding in the evening shadows. The caption reads, "And thus is born this weird figure in the dark . . . This avenger of evil . . . *'The Batman'*."

The prose is quite flamboyant and romantic, and the figure of the Batman, with his mask, his purple and blue costume and batlike cape, is visually exciting. He is a symbol of the dark and mysterious forces which work for good in the world, yet which have a menacing and dreadful side to them. The Batman's goal is to fight evil by creating *terror* in the hearts of criminals and to outlast them in battle. Bruce Wayne, we must remember, is an aristocrat; a wealthy man motivated by a desire for personal vengeance and perhaps by a sense of *noblesse oblige* to labor for mankind.

He is not a superior alien nor a mutant, like many other comic book heroes; instead he represents a highly developed human being, in terms of muscular strength and intellectual ability. Thus he is an aristocrat not only because of his wealth but also in terms of his development. As such he represents a model of what we all might become. Superman is beyond our highest expectations because of his fantastic origin; but Batman is not.

When he takes on his disguise he becomes a grotesque, a macabre figure whose sacred mission is to battle other grotesques. The Joker, his most significant nemesis, is a pathological murderer with hideous chalk-white face, green hair, and a maniacal grin on his face. Bob Kane introduces the Joker as follows:

> Once again a master criminal stalks the city streets—a criminal weaving a web of death about him—leaving stricken victims behind wearing a ghastly clown's grin—the sign of death from the JOKER! Only two dare to oppose him . . . BATMAN and ROBIN the boy wonder! Two to battle the grim jester called . . . the JOKER! A battle of wits . . . with swift death, the only compromise!!!

The Joker is described elsewhere in the story as having "burning, hate-filled eyes," "a smile of death," and as being "diabolical." In the story reprinted in *The Great Comic Book Heroes,* he announces his plans and executes them, despite precautions taken by the police, through ingenious ploys.

It seems obvious that the Joker is death—or an emissary of death, with his skeletal face and inhuman grin. Kane presents us with a world of fiends and grotesques, many of whom are connected in some way with animals (such as The Penguin). Implicit in all this is the notion that evil is, somehow, not part of the scheme of things; that it is associated with various kinds of unusual and diabolical freaks.

Kane's grotesques do not have the morbidity of Gould's

(*Dick Tracy*). Batman's adventures are not pervaded by the sense of passion that we find in the character of Dick Tracy, even though Batman is supposedly motivated by a desire for revenge. This is because Kane does not have the same sense of motivation as Gould. There is actually some question as to Kane's role in *Batman*. According to Ted White in "The Spawn of M.C. Gaines" (in *All in Color For a Dime*):

> *Batman* was not Kane's idea; it was dreamed up in an editorial session. Kane did not write the first story; it was written by either Gardner F. Fox or Bill Finger (reports vary). If Kane even drew the early stories, it was with considerable help from artists like Jake Cole (*Plastic Man*), Jerry Robinson, and Bob Wood (*Daredevil*). By the time of its early success, the stories were being drawn by Robinson and his friends. Although Kane's name appeared on every story until the mid-sixties (and the birth of the "New Look" Batman), his sole function was to subcontract the inking and pencilling to other artists—and the subdivision of payments seemed to guarantee sub-standard art.

Such a situation would prevent a strip from having the kind of intensity found in *Dick Tracy*, which bears the stamp of Gould's beliefs and personality directly.

As one of the most significant comic book heroes launched after Superman (and remember Batman is a human being with no super-powers), Batman's symbolic significance is quite problematical. The strip is stiffly drawn and perhaps even amateurishly done, so the art work is of minor importance. The plots, as comic book plots go, are fairly involved and interesting. But nothing in *Batman* would lead us to suspect he would be so popular and have such an impact on the popular imagination—via television as well as the comics.

Batman is so important because he symbolizes, and represents in concrete, personalized ways, basic American beliefs. The most important of these is the belief in the pietist-perfectionist, the individual who makes it *his* duty to right all wrongs. Batman, motivated as he is by vengeance, is in many respects an American archetype, and probably the foremost representative of this type of belief in the comics.

If you recall, I mentioned that his origin tale takes but two pages, and not a full two pages of comics at that. Some thirty years of Bruce Wayne's development are covered in a trifling manner. This fits in quite well with the American's sense of having no past, of having escaped from history, tradition, institutions, and other aspects of European culture. Yet, having no past creates problems, for without a past it becomes very difficult to achieve a coherent sense of self. How does one act? What does one believe? Who does one imitate?

Psychiatrists talk about an affliction called "the archaic conscience," or "archaic superego" often found in people who were raised in permissive families. Not having any limits, any built-in restraints, people with an archaic superego often torture themselves with a million self-inflicted punishments as a way of assuaging the rather diffuse sense of guilt they possess. I would like to suggest that, culturally speaking, a society which has rejected the past and traditions is very much like a child which has been brought up permissively, with few guidelines or restraints. The sense of guilt becomes overwhelming. (See my analysis of *Dick Tracy* for a discussion of the role of separation of church and state in this matter.) Just as we torture ourselves as individuals as a result of our archaic consciences, so do we on a cultural level strive to become heroic perfectionists, to rid ourselves of a nagging sense of guilt.

Pietism-perfectionism has been described by William G. McLoughlin (in "Pietism and the American Character," *American Quarterly*, Spring, 1961) as:

> . . . the belief that every individual is himself responsible for deciding the rightness or wrongness of every issue (large or small) in terms of a higher moral law; that he must make this decision the moment he is confronted with evil; and having made his decision, he must commit himself to act upon it at once, taking every opportunity and utilizing every possible method to implement his decision not only for himself and in his own home or community but throughout the nation and the world.

This is the mentality behind the crusader, whether he be caped and costumed or not. McLoughlin suggests that one consequence of pietism has been that there is widespread guilt in America over our inability to live up to impossible ideals. If we are disturbed about the inevitable compromises we have to make in life and are upset by feelings of guilt, we can take some degree of pleasure in a heroic figure who redeems us by his magnificent actions. Batman, an orphan (culturally as well as personally, it seems), is free to wreak vengeance on evildoers, though he does have a semi-official status and cooperates with the police. Yet, the inadequacy of the police and normal methods of detection free him to be a transcendent figure. He is only part of society; the fact that he is masked and disguised gives him an element of freedom. He is also aided by his superhuman strength and technological genius. In a sense he has the best of both worlds—riches and esteem as a beneficent millionaire and action and glory as a crime-fighting hero.

He is an intermediary between a weak society and master criminals and, like most comic book heroes, often has world-historical significance. Batman functions as a macabre manifestation of our collective sense of inadequacy and guilt. He will help regenerate the world, and his heroic labors take a load off of our backs, so to speak. He tells us, ultimately, that we live in a moral and just universe and those who laugh at us and break our laws *ultimately* will pay for their transgressions.

Thus *Batman* helps ease our guilt for our sins of omission (we haven't fought evil as diligently as we should have) and helps satisfy and curb our various impulses (by showing us that we will pay for our crimes). The horrendous, absurd, and monstrous criminals he captures provide us, then, with a certain amount of relief. The adventures function as moral strictures which alleviate our guilt. Since we do not have parents who will tell us what we can and cannot do, we have to get some sense of our limitations somewhere; comic book heroes help us here. They also provide us with vicarious action and information. The fact that so many comic book heroes are kinds of "men" and have the suffix "man" in their names lends support for this notion. These paper heroes are our spiritual fathers; they are our first heroes—or were, until television developed in the forties—and they are still of considerable importance to us.

In 1966 *Batman* appeared on television and was a great success for a few years. It appeared twice a week, on Wednesday and Thursday evenings. The adventure would be started on Wednesday and finished on Thursday.

The series was a great put-on. As Adam West, the actor who played Batman, said in an interview with John Stanley in the San Francisco *Chronicle* (Datebook, Sunday, January 9, 1966):

> We're doing it satirically, but in a very special sense. It's satirical as far as tendency toward style. And certainly satirical as far as exaggeration and overstatement are concerned. But the rudiment here is to play with the truth. You might say my job is to make the overstatement as subtle as possible . . . I like to think of myself as nature's nobleman, with a sole desire to stamp out crime.

The series led to a terrible movie, featuring the actors from the television series, and then, after flooding the country with what was called "Batmania," it collapsed and faded away. One more craze down the drain—another one of nature's noblemen lost his appeal, for some reason.

Batman had a particular role to play at this period. While adults laughed at him, catching the overstatement and self-ridicule, children took him seriously and followed his adventures assiduously. I believe this ambiguous role he played reflected something interesting about American culture. For adults and for sophisticated types, who saw Batman as "camp," it was one more example of the death of the heroic. There were no heroes, and anyone who pretended to be one was not to be taken seriously.

Still for thousands of youngsters and for less sophisticated adults, heroism was still possible, and Batman, despite his self-mockery, was still a legitimate heroic figure. When literary scholars talk about the death of the heroic, they are dealing with a relatively narrow frame of reference. The comics (as well as detective stories and spy intrigues) did not, as they developed, reflect a feeling of man's impotence, alienation, or the absurdity of life.

There may even be a connection between the activism of large numbers of young people in American society now, who grew up with the comics and watched *Batman*, and the notion that evil can be fought and that paralysis is not man's natural state. In this respect, Adam West's belief that he represented one of nature's noblemen, whose function it was to stamp out crime, is not as silly as it might seem. To a great degree the images dominating high literature—of life as absurd (i.e., action is stupid), and the view of man as forever alienated from himself and others—are European. We may find ourselves in a society that does create grave problems as far as the psyche is concerned, and we may be alienated from ourselves and others, but the heritage of American thought is that we can overcome these problems—and any problems.

If, on one hand, we have been overconfident—believing

ourselves supermen who could fight our way out of any problem—our serious literature has gone to the other extreme, picturing man as absurd, pitiful, and a powerless victim of blind and stupid fate. Both sides are ultimately comic and tragically unrealistic. But at least readers of *Batman* have hope and without hope there is no salvation, even though there may be no salvation even with hope.

The final transmogrification has come with the development of relevant themes in Batman and Robin. As Michael Stern described things in "Relevance in the Comics" (S.F. *Chronicle*):

> Batman and Robin, those inseparables of old, have split up. Robin is off handling campus crises at college, while Batman fights crime by night and social ills by day as City Councilman and head of the Wayne Foundation. Alfred the Butler has retired, the Wayne mansion has been sold and the Batcave closed up, and those ostentatious symbols like the Batplane and Batcar have been scrapped. (Robin's social conscience swings into action in D.C.'s Teen Titans Mag, where he, Wonder Girl, Superboy, Batgirl and others work with ghetto kids.)

I will say more about the changes in the comics elsewhere, but I should point out that the movement of such heroes into present-day social and political considerations is not out of character. In essence, they have been updated and their perspectives broadened, but the fundamental impulse to fight crime and evil is there; it is just that they now have a sociological conception of man, closely tied to liberal political views.

POGO AND HIS FRIENDS IN
THE OKEFENOKKE SWAMPS:
A Study in the Irony of Democracy

In the book-bound versions of some of his adventures of Pogo the issues range from loyalty checks to political slander, from aesthetic standards to rent-control picketing. In general the people of Pogoland face these issues with a good deal of naiveté, and it often appears they are going to be exploited by Bridgeport the bear, or Tammany the tiger, or Deacon Mushrat, or by the cowbirds. In the end the "simple people" prevail, and the manipulators and exploiters are discomfited.
— REUEL DENNEY, *The Astonished Muse*

Pogo has frequently been described as the greatest or most significant contemporary American comic strip, and Walt Kelly, who draws the strip, has been seen as a "worthy successor" to George Herriman, the creator of *Krazy Kat*. (R.

Reitberger and W. Fuchs, *Comics: An Anatomy of a Mass Medium*).

There are certain obvious similarities between *Pogo* and *Krazy Kat:* both are animal strips and both use language in a lyrical and fantastic manner. In addition, both strips are irreverent and often frankly antagonistic toward figures of authority. But *Pogo* is much less abstract and surrealistic than *Krazy Kat* and much more concerned with current events.

Kelly is a satirist whose targets are the absurdities and aberrations in American politics and society. He is a democrat, in the broadest sense of the term, and has bravely and bipartisanly ridiculed political figures he dislikes from the late Senator Joseph McCarthy to the present Vice President, Spiro Agnew.

Kelly attacked McCarthy in a number of different episodes, portraying him as a lynx named Simple J. Malarkey. In one adventure Malarkey became involved with two nasty characters—Mole MacCaroney and Deacon Mushrat—in an "anti-bird" crusade designed to protect the swamp from unwelcome immigrants. This tale had episodes involving book burnings and attempts to smear (literally) innocent animals by sticking them in a pot of tar, and then feathering them—making them, in effect, birds.

This was a rather obvious attack on McCarthy (the caricature of him was superbly drawn) and the John Birch society, and considering the way the United States was swept by hysteria in those days it was a courageous act.

The final outcome of the anti-bird episode was significant. Deacon Mushrat, fearing trouble from Mole and Malarkey (who seemed to be conspiring against him), pushes Malarkey into the pot of tar. Shortly afterwards Malarkey pulls Mole in with him, and they both end up trying to kill one another—an ironic, but fitting, conclusion.

This element of irony is, I believe, basic to the American popular imagination. Since we are an egalitarian nation, we cannot have tragedy in the Aristotelian sense of the term—the fall of a person of high rank, such as a king, owing to some flaw. And so we rely on irony—or as Aristotle put it, peripeteia.

Reversal is a common element to irony—things tend to work out the opposite of the way they are planned. However, logic is never violated, as ironic reversals are structural and based in indirect ways upon the law of contradiction. People are the agents of their own destruction—they are their own worst enemies.

In this respect it is significant that Kelly named one of his books *Pogo: We Have Met the Enemy and He Is Us,* and said in the introduction to this book, "Man has turned out to be his own worst enemy." There seems to be an element of fatalism in the ironic stance; a sense that it is only a matter of time before man measures out the correct amount of rope and proceeds to hang himself.

There is a moral (and perhaps even metaphysical) dimension to the plot of the strip, which seems to have more importance than the characters themselves. This is in itself ironic, since Americans take pride in their individualism and see it as the cornerstone of their democratic institutions. Yet, if I am right, the popular imagination finds meaning and profundity in stories which have ironic resolu-

tions and in which personality and character are of secondary importance. There is even a further irony in the fact
that one of the most savage satirists in American works in a
medium which is generally considered to be childish.

Kelly's brilliant caricatures make his work very powerful. Caricature involves the grotesque and ludicrous representation of people by exaggerating their characteristic features and at the same time retaining their likeness. It is
essentially skeptical and suggests that "people are not what
they claim to be or seem to be."

In focusing upon distortions and exaggerations, carica-
ure is implicitly trying to restore a sense of normality. It
suggests what should be by showing the absurdity of what
is. When Kelly draws Spiro Agnew as a hyena and sports
with his alliterative rhetorical style, we have a multi-
leveled attack on him and the things that he stands for.
Agnew is deprived of dignity (and even of the human form)
and becomes a comic figure—or perhaps *more* of a comic
figure than Kelly believes him to be.

Caricature involves the humor of exposure and deval-
uation. "Look," Kelly is saying . . . "look at what Spiro
Agnew *really* is—a hyena (which also looks something like
an ass) who goes around saying things like 'Would I be a
reborn BLADUD to blain our blenched ball, our WORLD, our
SPHEROID? a BLAD of blackwort?' "

To make things even more ridiculous, Kelly dresses
Agnew in a comic military uniform something like that
worn by a Greek colonel. This uniform has totalitarian implications, and so, suggests Kelly, does Agnew.

Agnew, though he seems to be one of Kelly's favorite

victims, is not by any means the only one. There are rather savage portrayals of a number of political figures such as Richard Nixon, George Romney, Lyndon Baines Johnson, Bobby Kennedy, and Khrushchev. Kelly not only caricatures these people, but he also turns them into animals or figures which symbolize certain characteristics. Thus he presents George Wallace as a cock, Khrushchev as a pig, Bobby Kennedy as a wind-up toy man, and Lyndon Johnson as a long-horn steer.

Turning people into various animals and toys gives Kelly's work added punch, for in addition to ridiculing his victims' appearances, he is able to dehumanize them or depersonalize them, and suggest what kind of character they have—based upon general notions we have about the personalities of various animals. When Kelly portrays Eugene McCarthy as a kind of toy knight on horseback, it speaks volumes both about McCarthy's own view of himself and about his image—how the American public sees him.

Kelly plays his part perfectly by denying that there is any significance to be found in *Pogo*.

> Every once in a while some grinning gargoyle of a dedicated liberal searching for meaning, a professional liberal who believes in liberalism rather than in liberty, comes grinning at me with teeth set like a jack-o'-lantern and says, "Walter, tell me, what are you trying to do? What's behind the strip?" Such a man is a cryptologist.
>
> The answer is simple, but unacceptable to such questioners. I've hinted at it all along. I'm trying to have fun and make money at the same time. (*Ten Ever-Lovin' Blue-Eyed Years with Pogo*.)

It is difficult to quarrel with someone who utterly denies any serious purpose to his work. It leaves the people who are caricatured by Kelly with no one to attack in turn. For by complaining about his treatment by Kelly, he would be dignifying the insult as well as admitting that he bears a resemblance to a pig, a cock, or whatever. It should also be noted that Kelly is anti-ideological; while many of his targets are conservatives, he also castigates liberals for being more concerned with their ideology than with liberty. Nevertheless he is the darling of the liberals, who delight in his satirizations of conservative and reactionary (and perhaps even some radical) figures.

It should be evident by now that *Pogo* is not just a funny little fable meant for children; there is a basic animus to the strip. It is permeated by a deep-seated and all-pervasive sense of hostility. Kelly, masquerading as a genial and funny fellow, ridicules, derides, mocks, and taunts any number of people, practices, and institutions. Although many of the readers of the strip are children, who enjoy it for its narrative story telling, there can be no question but that the basic ambience of the strip is that of anger and aggression.

Quite likely many adults sense this, though they may not consciously recognize this hostility because of their notions about what one finds in comic strips. Also, they may agree with Kelly so that his free-floating hostility reflects and reinforces the free-floating hostility that characterizes the American public at large.

One source of this hostility is our individualistic ethos, which leads to a great deal of self-aggrandizement and competitiveness. As Karen Horney has remarked in *The Neurotic Personality of Our Time*:

> Hostility is inherent in every intense competition, since the victory of one of the competitors implies the defeat of the other. There is, in fact, so much destructive competition in an individualistic culture that as an isolated feature one hesitates to call it a neurotic characteristic. It is almost a cultural pattern.

This passage occurs in Horney's discussion of neurotic competitiveness, and she has much to say about the positive as well as negative aspects of the subject. However, her point is that our culture breeds hostility, which may become so intense in individuals as to become a neurosis.

In the last chapter of her book, "Culture and Neurosis," she suggests that the economic structure of our society exacerbates our hostile feelings:

> Modern culture is economically based on the principle of individual competition. The isolated individual has to fight with other individuals of the same group, has to surpass them and, frequently, thrust them aside. . . . The psychic result of this situation is a diffuse hostile tension between individuals.

This hostility is frequently hidden in our psyches, but, though masked, our hostility is active. And it is this hostility (in part) that makes us take delight in seeing the high and mighty brought low and ridiculed in Kelly's caricatures.

With this in mind, the title *We Have Met The Enemy*

and He Is Us now takes on an added meaning. Not only are we our own enemies, but also everyone is everyone else's enemy. In this book there is a story called "A Pig Is a Pig," which deals with the pollution problem. Kelly wishes to show that ordinary people (as well as big factories) contribute to pollution. During the course of the episode, which takes place in a junk yard, we find that Pogo and Albert the Alligator have both contributed to pollution. Pogo then says to Albert the alligator, "EVERYBODY'S at fault, ol' son? Albert replies, "I guess EVER'BODY!" The sheriff then arrives at the scene and yells, "EVERYBODY'S GUILTY! EVERYBODY'S UNDER ARREST!"

The epidode is not meant to be a statement about man's moral status, but the psychological mechanisms at work all fit into place beautifully. The free-floating hostility and aggression, which damns everyone, now turns upon the self, leading to feelings of guilt. We find ourselves in a bind —we feel guilty if we are too competitive and successful, and we feel guilty if we do not compete and do not achieve what we feel (or are supposed to be) capable of achieving.

Pogo, and other strips like it, enable us to assuage these feelings of guilt and hostility by projecting them onto make-believe characters or caricatures from the political world and society at large. The dialogue in Pogo has what Denney calls an oral aggressive nature; people are parodied mercilessly in brilliant rhetorical passages. Kelly's caricatures represent a graphic attack on people; their features are distorted and they are portrayed as animals of one sort or another. In addition to the narrative structure and underlying irony of the strip, Kelly taunts almost everyone and makes them act in essentially self-destructive ways.

The swamp is portrayed as a primitive paradise that is under attack from all kinds of destructive types—mealy-mouthed religious fakes, confidence men, political cranks, and many other bad types. Even the natural inhabitants have their faults—Albert the alligator has cannibalistic tendencies; Churchy La Femme, the turtle, is a fool; Prof. Howland Owl is a mad scientist, and so forth.

All of this is masked and not evident, especially if you read *Pogo* daily in the newspaper. However, if you read various collections of *Pogo,* and get a sense of Kelly's work as a whole, I think you will find that there is much more to *Pogo* than meets the eye. It is rather uneven; at times it is dull and at other times simply remarkable. *Pogo* is not an easy strip to read and follow—it takes a good deal of effort, a certain amount of sagaciousness, and good eyesight.

The final irony of *Pogo* is the final irony of our democracy—our sense of equality is too often, it seems, little more than the guarantee that each of us will get an equal share and fair measure of hostility. Each and every person is both the source and subject of this hostility. And that focuses attention on the danger of equality—we will tolerate few differences (other than appearances) and, so it seems, no distinctions whatsoever.

PEANUTS
The Americanization of Augustine

His heroes are not animals but preschool-age children, "led" by Charlie Brown, whose faith in human nature (and in that of his little comrades) is always cruelly deceived. His chief tormentor is a scowling, cynical little girl, a real child shrew, named Lucy van Pelt. Linus, Lucy's brother, is a precocious, delicate intellectual whose nerves give way with the loss of the blanket he always carries around with him to reassure himself. Schroeder, whose greatest pleasure is to play Beethoven on his toy piano; the dirty Pig-Pen, and several others complete this childish team, to which must be added Snoopy, the hedonistic young puppy who is very pleased with living.

COUPERIE AND HORN, *A History of the Comic Strip*

Charles Schulz, the creator of *Peanuts,* is a rather shy person who personifies the American Dream. When he was graduating from high school, he saw an ad for an art school on a match-book cover. He sent away for information, took the course, and what do you know—he now makes more than three million dollars a year. Schulz used to be what we would now call "straight"—a crew-cut, clean-living mid-westerner, dedicated to his family and his religion.

That was before the exploitation and the commercialization of the strip reached its present stage. *Peanuts* is now so ubiquitous that it is literally part of the fabric of modern American society, and Schulz is the spokesman for millions of mute Americans. This success has had its effect on "Sparky" (as he is known to his friends), and his image is now much cooler. His hair is longer, he wears tinted aviator glasses, and was recently separated from his wife. But the strip remains the same.

Because the comic strip does not have much status as an art form, and because the characters in *Peanuts* are little children and a dog, we tend to underestimate Schulz's achievement, even though almost everybody admires his work. *I believe that Schulz is one of the greatest humorists of the twentieth century.* Over the course of some two dozen years of drawing the strip (it started in 1950) and thinking up the gags, he has developed a distinctive style of art work, an incredible assortment of characters, and a positively amazing command of the techniques of humor.

His *ouvrage* is monumental. And though his earlier work was not particularly exceptional, he has developed his talent to an extraordinary level over the years. We find his work all about us—on school lunch boxes, on sheets and pillowcases, on dolls, calendars, in the theater, and on television. The strip is also popular abroad—some hundred million people read it daily—though I believe it is essentially American in its spirit.

We enjoy *Peanuts* because it is extremely funny. Schulz mixes graphic, verbal, and ideational humor in a genuinely inventive manner. He is a master of representing expressions in his characters. His characters tend to be monomaniacs who pursue their destinies with all the zany abandon of divinely inspired zealots. We seldom see them this way, however, because we have been taught to regard children (and dogs) as innocent and mildly amusing.

Schulz does not accept this notion; he portrays children in all their Augustinian corruptness. The characters in *Peanuts* exist after the fall of man from the Garden of Eden. They are corrupted by original sin and therefore can be selfish egoists without any strain on our credulity.

There are no adults in the strip; there are no authority figures, though Lucy, by virtue of her domineering personality and ready resort to fisticuffs, is probably the locus of power for all practical purposes. The strip is a fascinating study in anarchy. Without any central organizing power to set limits and establish boundaries, we find a collection of self-important petty sovereigns—or perhaps petty tyrants. A peanut is an "insignificant or tiny person," and Schulz's characters are in reality peanuts in both senses of the word. As far as their self-image is concerned, however, they are giants.

They are also lovable. Guilt does not make people nasty or hateful. Robert L. Short explains this in his analysis of "Original Sin" in *The Gospel According to Peanuts:*

First of all, the doctrine of Original Sin (including the Garden of Eden story) is not so much concerned with *how* the human predicament got the way it is, as it is concerned to show *what* the human predicament is. And what is the "human predicament"? Is it that each one of us, every man born of a woman, is *born* under the *curse* of sin ("A curse comes to being/As a child is formed"), that we all have our personal origins in sin, that we all *originate* this way in life— and hence the term "*Original* Sin." (This is also why some churches call Original Sin, "Birth-Sin.") But this sinfulness does not necessarily manifest itself in meanness or hatefulness. . . .

Just the opposite, in fact, may be the case. A man who accepts sin as a reality of the human condition has a much more philosophical attitude toward man's frailities than the man who sets a standard of sin-free perfection. Consequently, he is more understanding in human relations.

The love in *Peanuts* is based upon understanding, not illusion; Schulz is a supreme realist. One of the strip's charms is that it openly acknowledges pride and stupidity and gullibility and all the other evil qualities (or nasty ones) in man, and still is able to be accepting. Somehow we all feel that Schulz accepts man for what he is, not what he claims to be. Schulz relieves us of the awesome burden of innocence, and we are all grateful.

Schulz's characters are only innocent in the sense they are asexual and pregenital; they have all the vices of adults in every other aspect. They are subject to passions, susceptible to whims, motivated by greed or love, and they never learn. Lucy pursues Shroeder relentlessly, never understanding (or admitting to herself) that he does not particularly like her. Linus is insecure, and an emotional cripple without his blanket. Charlie Brown is continually suffering ignominious defeats on the baseball diamond and is victimized by people who take advantage of his trusting nature.

Since the characters are children (and animals), we are not offended by the light they throw on our vices. Naive commentators have long been used as a literary device by humorists to point out our shortcomings. Huck Finn is a case in point. But Twain's humor has a savage intensity, founded on a sense of moral outrage that we do not find in Schulz, whose satire is infinitely more gentle and genial. Schulz deals with a wider perspective and operates at a higher level of abstraction.

Peanuts is a commentary on the human condition, from the perspective of a person who understands human nature and man's invincible ignorance and propensity toward folly. The comic strip format does not easily lend itself to the more biting satire of Twain or Swift, but it does lend itself to satire and social commentary, and Schulz is probably the king of popular psychologists and lighthearted critics of man in America.

And though we are exposed to Schulz in bits and pieces, one strip per day, over the years the characters have taken on a certain identity—so that their adventures have more meaning to us after we have followed them for a number of years. All of the characters have changed too. They have not grown older (that is a convention of the comic strip); but as Schulz has perfected his style, they

have changed their appearance and developed their personalities considerably. As I pointed out earlier, the first strips
were rather bland. Schulz had not yet developed his characters nor mastered the techniques of humor.

An important element behind humor—an insight we
get from Freud and psychoanalysis—is that it serves to
mask aggression. The energy that we expend laughing at
the ridiculous releases pent-up hostilities. Under the guise
of wit, Schulz says things we would rather not hear. He
does this by defining things in an amusing way. "Happiness," he tells us, "is a warm puppy;" or "happiness is feeling the wind and rain in your hair." These definitions,
which have a folksy quality to them, are really like proverbs
—and Schulz is following a long line of humorists in America from Benjamin Franklin on, who cloaked their moralizing in witty phrases and comic maxims. Humor is implicitly social, and we must expect a certain amount of
moralizing from our humorists. Proverbs, really, are moral
directives. Schulz disguises this ethical element in his work
so beautifully that we seldom see it.

Snoopy, from atop his doghouse, is very much a com-
mentator from a mock-pulpit, calling man to see his errors
and return to the straight and narrow path. In one episode,
Snoopy has allowed four homeless birds to use his doghouse
as a temporary refuge. They become so noisy playing bridge
that Snoopy has to drive them away (the last one carrying a
little bridge table on his head). Snoopy then comments: "A
Friend is NOT someone who takes advantage of you!"
There is something about being on doghouses, pulpits or

even soapboxes that brings out the moralist in man—and dogs like Snoopy.

Schulz is a mirthful moralist; he continues to point out our frailties and calls upon us to lead the good life. His particular instrument is his comic genius and the remarkable collection of many characters he has created in his strip. He does not sentimentalize childhood, and perhaps goes a step or two in the opposite direction at times, but then childhood is a period with many bitter and painful experiences.

Peanuts does a number of things for us. It points out, by implication, the danger of a society full of egoists who pursue their particular passions; it offers us little homilies and morality plays to help us maintain our righteousness; it offers us insights into the many frailties of man and human nature; and it enables us to release our aggressions by having a remarkable assortment of comic characters and fools for us to laugh at. It is no wonder that the strip is so popular with adults, for it is very reassuring. It says, "Don't feel so guilty about your children! Children are born with guilt, and people are fools anyway!" This relieves adults of a great deal of responsibility, and justifies the occasional feelings of anger and hostility people may feel toward their children.

Actually, *Peanuts* is full of inversions. We find children who act like adults, dogs who act like humans, and a comic strip which deals with many of the profundities of life and does not sentimentalize children. Inversion is also central to the pastoral, and I believe we must understand *Peanuts* as a kind of pastoral. When we think of the pastoral, we usual-

PEANUTS
by
SCHULZ

HERE'S THE WORLD WAR I PILOT TAKING OFF FROM A FIELD SOMEWHERE IN ENGLAND...

DRAT THIS FOG! IT'S BAD ENOUGH HAVING TO FIGHT THE RED BARON WITHOUT FIGHTING THE FOG, TOO!

HEADQUARTERS EXPECTS MUCH OF US...WHEN I (BACK, I THINK I'LL WRIT LETTER TO PRESIDENT WIL

BRUISED AND BATTERED I CRAWL OUT OF MY WRECKED SOPWITH CAMEL... I'M TRAPPED IN THE MIDDLE OF NO-MAN'S LAND! SLOWLY I CREEP FORWARD...

SUDDENLY, THERE IT IS..... BARBED WIRE !!! I'VE GOT TO GET THROUGH IT BEFORE THE MACHINE GUNNERS SEE ME..

2-6

ly imagine shepherds and maidens frolicking on the grass. But in its modern manifestations we can interpret the pastoral as a device which uses inversion and puts the complex into the simple. Schulz's children act like adults in a society where adults often act like children.

There is a certain abstract quality to the strip. The characters do not seem to live in society, *per se*—though society is intimated in the form of schools and psychiatrists and holidays. Much of the action takes place beyond society in a state of nature, with modern shepherds and shepherdesses playing out their roles.

I have, in the course of this discussion, described Schulz's characters as *fools*. There are many aspects of the various characters which are foolish, as the dictionary defines fool:

> A person lacking in judgment or prudence; a retainer formerly kept in great households to provide casual entertainment and commonly dressed in motley with cap, bells and bauble; one who is victimized or made to appear foolish (a dupe).

Certainly Snoopy and Charlie Brown and Linus and all the other characters have this element about them. But in addition they have a certain inflexibility in their character which verges on monomania and becomes the central element of their foolishness. Their obsessions are patently absurd, and it is this rather mechanical rigidity that does a great deal to create the humor in the strip.

In *The Anatomy of Criticism,* Northrop Frye explains how the humor of characterization works. He points out that there are four basic comedy types:

1. *alazones* or imposters
2. *eirons* or self-deprecators
3. *bomolochoi* or buffoons
4. *agroikos* or churls

The basis of comedy, which he says frequently deals with defeated characters, is:

> a victory of arbitrary plot over consistency of character. Thus, in striking contrast to tragedy, there can hardly be such a thing as inevitable comedy, as far as the action of the individual play is concerned. That is, we may know that the convention of comedy will make some kind of a happy ending inevitable, but still for each play the dramatist must produce a distinctive "gimmick" or "weenie," to use disrespectful Hollywood terms. . . .

Schulz's genius, then, is in finding ways of manipulating his stock characters so that unexpected resolutions occur or that the resolutions that we anticipate do not occur.

He is aided by the fact that we all learn certain conventions as we are socialized, and by the fact that the characters—after a while—take on a comic dimension regardless of what they do. At a certain point the pattern takes over, and we decide (on the unconscious level) that whatever the characters do is funny. As Frye says ". . . laughter is partly a reflex, and like other reflexes, it can be conditioned by a simple repeated pattern." That explains in part the significance of the compulsive nature of

Schulz's characters (and most other comic characters)—they are a means toward conditioning us to laugh.

By all odds the greatest of Schulz's characters, and the one he relies most upon, is Snoopy. Snoopy is the latest and one of the greatest manifestations of the talking animal convention. Not only does he talk, but he has a brilliant personality—he carries on human relationships, he is a *bon vivant,* he participates in history, he has an incredible imagination, he is witty, he expresses himself with virtuosity in any number of ways (eye movements, ear movements, tail movements, wisecracks, facial expressions), and he is superb as mimic and dancer. He has energy and spirit and a heart overflowing with kindness, though he has been known to boot a bird or two, or snatch a blanket.

There is, in fact, an existential dimension to Snoopy. He is an existential hero in every sense of the term. He strives, with dogged persistence and unyielding courage, to overcome what seems to be his fate—that he is a dog; that he is *just* a dog. And somehow he does it! I think we see Snoopy as a "person" who happens to be a dog, rather than a dog who happens to become a person—as is the case in Mikhail Bulgakov's brilliant satire *Heart of a Dog.*

"Existence precedes essence" says the distinguished French philosopher Jean-Paul Sartre—and if Snoopy's existence is that of a human is it not reasonable to think of him as one? Dogs don't fight the Red Baron or cruise around in dark glasses looking for chicks in the dorms. Nor do dogs write novels or develop phobias.

What Snoopy demonstrates, to all his readers, is that ultimately we are all free to create ourselves as we wish, no matter what our status on the Great Chain of Being might be. We can all be authentic if only we will have the courage *to* be what we can be. And this applies even to dogs.

Snoopy is an animal who has transcended his limitations, though he still has some. How curious that in a society characterized (so many social scientists tell us) by a growing sense of alienation and apathy, a dog in a comic strip is just bursting with *joie de vivre,* vitality, and hope. Perhaps we have reached the stage in which we live vicariously through Snoopy—and all the other characters in the strip. This is the ultimate inversion—a multitude of lifeless (in the sense of being de-energized and neurasthenic) and mute humans leading a kind of vicarious existence in the lives of comic strip characters . . . as well as through other entertainments offered by the mass media.

This is somewhat farfetched, but there is little question in my mind that one of the reasons for the popularity of *Peanuts* is that it helps assuage our hunger for *personality* in a world that is full of dehumanizing forces and in which identity is so much under attack. Snoopy shows that man's spirit has resiliency and that there is hope yet.

Schulz has said that his greatest ambition is to create a comic strip as good as *Krazy Kat,* probably the greatest comic strip produced to date. There is little question, I think, that he has come close to this goal. Schulz has transformed a comic strip into part of the very essence of American life. Charlie Brown and Linus and Snoopy and their cohorts are not just comic strip characters; they have long since transcended their roles and now are part of the galaxy of great comic creations, in any form of popular art. His characters have become legends in their own comic strip lifetimes.

PART III

THE AGE OF CONFUSION

THE THIRD GENERATION OF COMICS

By the time you come to *Zap* comics and *The Fantastic Four,* you are in a different world from that of the innocents and even from that of the Modern Age comics. Comics are now explicity political and sexual—characters become pregnant and have children, and in some comics spend a good deal of time copulating. There is also a radical thrust to many comics now, as heroes and superheroes tackle such problems as ecology, racism, the Vietnam war, frigidity, and alienation.

We find a break with Puritanism and yet, as I point out in my analysis of what I call "eroticomics," there is a diffuse kind of Puritanism beneath all the sensuality and licentiousness. Whether the exuberance and sense of exhilaration reflected in the contemporary comics—which start roughly with the sixties—will continue or whether these comics are just a fad that will fade remains to be seen.

For the moment it is fair to say they reflect a bewildering sense of freedom from social limitations and a fascination with the body (physical as well as political). They mirror a culture which is confused and uncertain about itself and the future.

MARVEL COMICS

Machines, Monsters, and the Myth
of America

The machines and monsters found in *The Fantastic Four**
have direct relevance to the relationship existing between
technology and American culture, a subject of considerable
importance. A glance at *The Fantastic Four* shows that the
creators of these works are fascinated with large, hulklike
creatures as well as fantastic machines. The pages abound
with "Hulks" and "Things"—*grotesques* which are unnatu-
ral in shape and appearance—ugly, fantastic and incongruous.

---

* This team is made of the following personalities: Reed Richards, a scientific
genius who can stretch his limbs like rubber; Sue Storm Richards, Reed's wife
who can make herself invisible and throw a force field; Johnny Storm, The
Human Torch; Ben Grimm, The Thing, who supposedly has the "greatest natural power" in the world. Stan Lee writes the stories and Jack Kibby does the
art work.

On the visual level alone the grotesque is significant. Its ugliness is an affront to society and suggests that something is wrong with the social order. Just as a caricature is an attack on an individual, by means of distorting some feature of a person (while keeping resemblance), so is a grotesque an attack upon society. The distortion and ugliness of the grotesque symbolizes all that is wrong and ugly in the society which created the grotesque. As William Van O'Connor points out in *The Grotesque: An American Genre,* "the grotesque afronts our sense of established order and satisfies, or partly satisfies, our need for at least a tentative, a more flexible ordering."

(I would not claim that the readers of Marvel Comics or of Faulkner, for that matter, are conscious of the way the grotesque works, but I do believe that on a subconscious level they do respond to the grotesque in the way I have indicated.)

In *The Strategy of Desire* Ernest Dichter, the well-known motivational researcher, offers some interesting ideas on the psychological significance of the monsters—based on extensive surveys he conducted. The monster, Dichter claims, functions in a rather complex way upon our psyche:

> They fascinate us because they show us forces out of control. What is horrifying is that the uncontrollable monster is, in many aspects, really ourselves. What is fascinating is that we would not mind being a little bit out of control every once in a while, if only just to redress the balance.

Dichter made a study of responses to horror films, but his

conclusions can be applied to comics since the same mechanisms are at play. These works:

> are really concerned with the origins, the forces, the uses of
> power, and the evil and guilt which are a consequence of its
> use: the power of the creator—*Frankenstein;* the power of
> omnipotence—*The Invisible Man;* the power of brutishness—
> *King Kong;* the power of knowledge—*Dr. Jeckyll and Mr.*
> *Hyde;* the power of resurrection—*Dracula.*

It is his theory that society cannot act with proper speed to
control these monsters because society *itself* is guilty. It
must share responsibility for the existence of these monsters; it fails to appreciate their essential humanity, and it
recognizes, in its heart, that it is very much like the monster itself.

Dichter sees several ambivalent forces at work in the
perceptions of the monsters, in the society represented in
the horror films, (or comics) and in the audiences. The
monster, usually the victim of a cosmic trick, never can be
certain where the seat of the evil resides—in himself or his
creator? Ultimately, he destroys himself:

> At the end, perceiving his own monstrosity in the faces of his
> victims, he is taken in by their perceptions. He becomes the
> cause of his own undoing.
>
> The other two ambivalent forces are society as it is represent-
> ed in the film and the audience watching the film. In the
> form of the monster they have the vicarious and powerful
> expression of their own grudges against the powers that be; in
> the form of the monster's eventual punishment they have the

vicarious and powerful expression of their own disapproval of their own impulses.

What all this means, then, is that the various monsters we find in *The Fantastic Four* provide us with the means for working through our aggressions in a rather sophisticated manner. Comic books are not exactly like films, but they function in much the same way.

Despite the apparent simplicity of the comic book, in which there is generally some kind of a conflict between a superhero and a monster, these tales provide readers both with an outlet for hostile and aggressive tendencies *and* with a way of learning to control them.

In addition to this psychological function, the monsters in our comics tell us something about our dominant concerns and fears, which show up in the *kinds* of grotesques we create and the adventures in which they are involved. In Marvel Comics we find a curious tendency to merge the human and the machine into super-technological entities. The powers of *The Fantastic Four* tend to be natural: The Thing supposedly has the "greatest human force" in the universe; other members of the team can turn into fire, become invisible, throw out fields of force or stretch— though Reed Richards is himself a scientific genius and can come up with devices to counter the various mad scientists who appear from time to time.

The villains generally cannot match the natural power of *The Fantastic Four* and are forced to rely on technology. Such is the case with Dr. Doom, whose mother was a witch and who learned strange mystic secrets from Tibet as well

as the scientific knowledge of the Western world. Quasimo-
do, a machine who is made human by The Silver Surfer,
and Psychoman are further examples.

We find a considerable difference in attitude (as far as
science and technology are concerned) in the works of our
elite artists and our popular artists. The comic book and
the novel point out these extremes. The dominant thrust of
high literature has been a revulsion against science and the
machine. Novelists and poets generally see science and
technology as a threat to humanity and recoil against it almost in panic. Thus most contemporary utopian novels are
dystopies which see societies of the future as totalitarian
and antihuman.

This is due, in part, to a bias in our higher arts, which
have traditionally looked toward nature for a source of in-
spiration and wisdom. *The Fantastic Four* reflect a much
different attitude toward science. Although the various villains are able to use science and technology for their evil
purposes, *they are always defeated by heroes who are superior morally and technologically.* Rather than refusing to
see the possibilities opened by technology, literary forms
such as comic books use science for their subject matter.
The victories of the good guys express a fundamental American optimism and reflect an awareness of the potentialities
for good and evil in machines and a belief in man's ability
to control them. Thus, comic strips have a realistic awareness of the moral dilemma posed by science and technology.

This awareness is evident in an adventure entitled
"This Man . . . This Monster" (June, 1951). Here, a machine is given an entire page. There is a sense of threat from

the very size of the device, a "radical cube" which dwarfs the figures who are to use it, and from its function: that of sending people into "subspace." How ominous! But the cube is to gain information on the space-time principle which is needed to defend the earth and the human race, so its size is secondary in importance to its purpose. *The Fantastic Four* are, in their own way, larger than lifesize, thus the cube becomes even less menacing.

The machine sends Richards into subspace, which is represented by a rather magnificent full-page spread of worlds, galaxies, and space. The presentation of landscape is particularly interesting in *The Fantastic Four*. The artist, Kirby, creates brilliant panoramas of gothic castles or modern super megalopolae with remarkable flair and a wonderful sense of spatiality. The settings for the adventures tend to be either urban or primitive, and in both, extremes tend to dominate. The urban developments sometimes take on modernistic, utopian characteristics and are as far removed from the "wild nature" scene as can be imagined. Generally speaking, the adventures are played out in some kind of an urban setting, suggesting an acceptance in the "sub-literary" mind of the city as the environment for modern man.

But what relation do these machines and monsters have to the myth of America? The "myth of America" is, itself, hard to pin down, and numerous secondary myths make it even more elusive. But we do have a number of references to the "myth of America" such as that offered by D.H. Lawrence in *Studies in Classic American Literature:*

The leatherstocking novels . . . go backwards, from old age to golden youth. That is the true myth of America. She starts old, old, wrinkled and writhing in an old skin. And there is a gradual sloughing of the old skin towards a new youth. It is the myth of America.

Lawrence saw the myth embodied in the figure of Cooper's Deerslayer:

> He is neither spiritual nor sensual. He is a moralizer, but he always tried to moralize from experience, not from theory. He says: "Hurt nothing unless you're forced to." Yet he gets his deepest thrill of gratification, perhaps, when he guts a bullet through the heart of a beautiful buck, as it stoops to drink at the lake. Or when he brings the invisible bird fluttering down in death, out of the high blue. "Hurt nothing unless you're forced to." And yet he lives by death, by killing the wild things of the air and earth.
>> It's not good enough.
> But you have there the myth of the essential white America. All the other stuff, the love, the democracy, the floundering into lust, is a sort of by play. The essential American soul is hard, isolate, stoic, and a killer. It has never yet melted.

For Lawrence nature did not lead to the good democrat and automatic progress, as most students of the myth of America insisted it has, but this is beside the point. *The idea that America represents a new start, where history, institutions, and complexity can be left behind seems to be the essence of our myth.* An antithesis is established between what America stands for—innocence, hope, individualism, simplicity, will, equality, democracy, etc.—and Europe. How do the machines and monsters in *The Fantastic Four* relate to the myth of America? What do they tell us about this myth as far as the viewpoint of the millions who read Marvel Comics is concerned?

For one thing we find in *The Fantastic Four* a recognition of the inadequacy of innocence as a stance—and of its high social cost: namely paralysis. This means that nature is not seen as beneficent in all cases, and goodness is not to be measured *solely* in terms of closeness to nature. How can it, when nature can produce *monsters* or men who will create monsters? These comics reflect an ambivalent feeling about nature: it is the source of evil as well as good, it is necessary (the power of *The Fantastic Four* tends to be natural) but not sufficient (Reed Richards is a technological genius).

Second, these works are intellectual (to the degree that science fiction can be intellectual). Many argue that science fiction just plays around with technological gadgetry but doesn't really exhibit the kind of thinking found in science or understand what science is about. I'm not so sure that this is always the case. But what is at issue here is not whether science fiction writers understand science but how they (and their public) feel about it. A radical cube may be bad science; however, it reflects an attitude about science that is quite positive but not worshipful! Progress is a function of intelligence as well as moral character, and not simply a matter of rejecting European culture and society.

Third, we find a definite expression of optimism in these stories—both in the events which take place and in their very form. In Joseph Frank's celebrated essay, "The Meaning of Spatial Form," there is a discussion of the theories of Wilheim Worringer, whose ideas are relevant to this discussion. According to Worringer, there is a continual alternation of naturalistic and non-naturalistic art styles, which are determined by man's sense of his place in the cosmos. In naturalistic periods man feels himself part of nature and able to dominate it, and his art work reproduces the forms of nature. When man feels he is not in harmony with nature he develops nonorganic, linear, and geometric forms. If Worringer is correct, the comic books (as well as Pop Art, for instance) reflect a basic confidence in man's ability to dominate the forces of technology and industrialization. For every fantastic monster or problem we find an ingenious solution and hero. Despite the violence and terror in the comics they display an underlying optimism about man's possibilities. We may question, then, whether this really is an age of the antihero? It may be for many writers and artists, but it does not seem to be the case for millions of Americans.

EROTICOMICS

or "What Are You Doing with that
Submachine Gun, Barbarella?"

There is in the comics a great deal of passion and sometimes a good deal of sex. Allow me to let the cat out of the
bag right away—one of the main reasons people read (or
should I say "look at"?) comics is that comics are suffused
with eroticism. In all their various manifestations (strips,
comic books, hardcover collections), the comics provide
some of the best girl-watching around.

Most sociologists and psychologists have been so preoc-
cupied with violence and horror in the comics that they
tend to neglect the eroticism in them.

Think about it for a minute. It is perfectly logical—and
natural—to find eroticism in the comics, since we find erot-

ic elements in all art forms. Man is to a great degree a *scopophile* (literally, a "looking lover"—one who derives sexual gratification from gazing at nudes) and has been for thousands of years. In the Middle Ages a favorite story format involved the "conversion" of the Saracen maiden. The great appeal of this story was that the maiden had to be baptized, and the descriptions of her disrobing (and her physical attributes) for baptism were lovingly detailed and most comprehensive. One way or another, man has displayed a genius for figuring out ways to get clothes off women.

With our graphic art forms we can now serve the same psychic needs more directly and do so for a wider audience. Until the development of the mass media and general literacy, not many people had access to works of art, whether it be books, paintings, sculpture, or the like. But man has always been a bawdy animal, and this is reflected in his literature as well as in his art. Some spark in man has always fought against the almost overwhelming repression caused by society. In this respect, obscenity can be looked upon as a mark of our humanity; only man believes that there is such a thing as obscenity or divinity—and uttering obscenities is a gesture of sorts that we make in the face of pressures toward conformity and depersonalization.

In the lusty Middle Ages prostitutes went into churches in search of customers and on certain festival days obscene pictures were sold—the immoral equivalent, I imagine, of the dirty pictures for which Paris is (or was) famous. And such works as Boccaccio's *The Decameron,* Shakespeare's plays, and I could go on and on, all have an erotic and ribald nature. It is only logical, then, to find eroticism in the comics; and we do.

Once this is established we must ask: What does it mean? Aside from the observation that comics are often erotic, what can we learn from these comics other than that voyeurs will be voyeurs?

We must first make a distinction between eroticism in the daily comics, which is just one aspect of these comics, and the overtly and conspicuously erotic, perhaps even pornographic, comics (the eroticomics) we find in books such as *Jodelle* or *Barbarella,* or recent comics books such as *Zap.*

In the everyday comic there is a good deal of rather innocent display. We see Tiffany Jones's cleavage and occasionally her breasts. How convenient it is that she is a model who spends a good deal of her time dressing and undressing. In another English comic strip, *Jane,* we often see Jane completely nude, caught in one embarrassing (notice how close the word "embarrassing" is to "bare ass"?) situation after another.

There are a lot of pretty girls to be seen, and in some cases the drawings are themselves remarkably sensual. Here the Italian comic strip artist Guido Crepax is outstanding. He peoples his strips with gorgeous, long-stemmed beauties in various stages of dress and undress, and breaks up the block format of the comic page in an interesting manner. His art work brings the comic strip very close to high fashion, but the eroticism is tangential to the story and somewhat diffuse.

In all of these strips the erotic aspects are incidental;

they are just one element (though an important one). Over the past few years, however, we can trace the development of comics that are consciously erotic, the eroticomics, the best known of which is *Barbarella*. But *Barbarella* is not the best eroticomic by a long shot.

Barbarella is a French comic strip heroine who looks somewhat like Brigitte Bardot and is involved in a number of erotic adventures in outer space, during which she often loses her clothes and bares her pointed breasts (almost literally) at the universe. She is not coy at all.

There is a scene, for example, which shows her naked, her hair tousled, lying in bed after what has obviously been a bit of lovemaking. She has that dreamy look on her face and her fleshy lower lip hangs down invitingly. "Diktor," she says to the robot who has just made love to her, "you have real style." "Oh! Madame is too kind," he replies. "I know my shortcomings. . . . There's something a bit mechanical about my movement."

How's that for Gallic wit? *Barbarella* is supposed to be a satire on comic heroines, science fiction, pornography, and many other things, but it lacks focus, isn't drawn very well, and gets to be a bore. It really isn't erotic, since Jean-Claude Forest, who did *Barbarella,* is relatively inhibited. There's little that's really juicy in the book. The same cannot be said for *Jodelle,* about a lusty wench whose sexual appetite is almost boundless. Barbarella is drawn in a somewhat realistic, though stiff, manner while Jodelle is consciously simplified and cartoon-like.

Aside from the various fantastic adventures they have, there is something both Jodelle and Barbarella have in common. They both are killers, and from time to time are shown shooting people with machine guns. This aspect of the strips has great cultural significance as a manifestation of certain unconscious attitudes men have about women. *We are ambivalent about them: they are a source of love and gratification, but they also are potentially destructive, and often use their beauty and sexuality to murder us.*

Curiously enough, we find the same thing in the Italian comic strip *Satanic,* where this theme of the beautiful woman who uses her sex to kill is literally and crudely portrayed. It is this ambivalent love-fear attitude that may, in fact, be a reason for the existence of eroticomics and other forms of eroticism. Men who fear women, yet need them, somehow solve the problem by substituting eroticism for the real thing.

The selections from *Jodelle* and *Satanic,* one of the new Italian *fummetti neri* (black comics), will benefit from scrutiny. In *Jodelle* we find that two girls have been caught by guards. The girls are lithe and tantalizing, with slightly open, almost pouting lips. The guards are rather brutish and elephantine, with huge arms and legs. Immediately upon being discovered, the girls slip off their clothes, revealing full breasts supported by relatively flimsy brassieres, which allow the top part of their nipples to show. The legionnaires take off the brassieres and there is a sexual orgy, in which the two girls accommodate a half dozen or so men.

After they have sexual relations, the men are shown as spent, sitting on the ground perspiring profusely with close-mouthed and rather vacuous faces, as if they had been drained of energy. Before they had sex they always were pictured smiling and laughing, with flashing teeth. The whites of their eyes have also disappeared. After the girls seize the weapons, all one sees is a fountain of blood. The last panel, which shows the nude girls with the machine guns, has almost an archetypical quality.

Satanic is about an old hag, a chemistry professor who transforms herself into a beautiful young lady and slaughters men with abandon. In one adventure she has lured an older man into following her up the steps of a temple, inducing a fatal heart attack. She is shown opening her dress and exposing her breasts to him. He is pictured as almost delirious with excitement—his eyes glaring, his body trembling, as he shouts, "I'm coming, I'm coming. . . ." The significance of the scene and the words is apparent. And the next panel, which shows her bending over a corpse with out-stretched arms and a grotesque death mask of a face, only reinforces the common fear that women only want to kill men and take their valuables. As she takes the money from his wallet she thinks, "This will come in handy." Indeed!

All of this is rather crudely done and perhaps even simpleminded. Yet the graphic presentation of such ideas must be significant—especially if you consider that *Satanic* and the other erotic horror comics are extremely popular, the biggest thing in Italian publishing in recent years. In fact, the very crudeness and childishness of these stories suggest that they must be particularly meaningful, since the artists and writers lack the ability to give their works any sophistication and are unable to hide or repress their dreams and fears.

The portrayal of women in eroticomics or pornographic

(whatever the word means) comics is not the same as in the innocent comics or girlie magazines. In the latter two cases women are shown in a much more positive light—as very desirable and wonderful. All of this leads me to conclude that what the eroticomics reveal, really, is a somewhat subliminal fear of sexuality; they are, in effect, graphic representations of the triumph of the *superego* in man, which says that if you open the Pandora's box of sexuality, you'll pay for it.

It might also be argued that these erotic books appeal to our infantile tendencies, and are pregenital: we get a certain kind of pleasure from them but they don't really satisfy, so we must continually return for more, so to speak. In many cases I would say this is true. Yet the ambience of many of these books, especially the American ones, suggests a rather relaxed, taken-for-granted attitude toward sex that really doesn't jibe with infantilism and social repression.

If you look, for example, at *Zap* comics (issue number four of which has been declared "pornographic" by the police in San Francisco), you see that they have a satiric quality. In a takeoff on a California motorcycle gang's adventure called "The Hog Ridin' Fools," the women are all quite ugly, but so are the men, and the hero of the story is a horny satyr-demon. In this story, as in *Barbarella* and *Jodelle,* the women are violent and punishing, though the story is so full of absurdity and nonsense that this violence doesn't *seem* particularly threatening.

But in all the comics I've been discussing women are menacing, and perhaps somewhat vampirish, using sex to weaken or kill men, or to get them off their guard so they can be killed with weapons. In these stories, there are important subconscious fears that come welling up.

The eroticomics we've looked at, for all their ribaldry and celebration of sexuality and carnality, are permeated by a deep-seated fear of women. We sense that women can use their bodies as weapons, so to speak, just as they allow their bodies to be used by advertisers to sell products. As Marshall McLuhan put it in his essay "The Mechanical Bride" (in the book of the same name):

> To the mind of the modern girl, legs, like busts, are power points which she has been taught to tailor, but as parts of the success kit rather than erotically or sensuously. She swings her legs from the hip with masculine drive and confidence. She knows that a "long-legged gal can go places." As such, her legs are not intimately associated with her taste or with her unique self but are merely display objects like the grill-work on a car. They are date-baited power levers for the management of the male audience.

What we find in the eroticomics is a thinly veiled fear that women can use their bodies to destroy men as well as manage, or perhaps manipulate, them. This is reinforced by the fact that often these lovely women are shown with guns and weapons—phallic symbols that they have expropriated and which they often use against men. There is certainly an element of castration anxiety here.

All of these considerations lead me to believe that, despite their superficial fascination with the body and titillation, eroticomics are, in essence, quite conscience-ridden. They reflect a fundamental and rather crushing anxiety that is hidden by their manifest content. They are, then, very puritanical! But don't tell that to the censors.

MR. NATURAL AND HIS FRIENDS FROM THE UNDERGROUND
Infantile Disorders of the Cerebellum and the Crotch

Underground comics, which have become quite popular in recent years, are hard to characterize. There are so many different kinds of underground comics and they try to do so many different things that just about the only thing they have in common is the way in which they are printed and distributed. Generally speaking, today's underground comics are part of the counterculture and are associated with underground newspapers, radical politics, and various movements that reject the basic value system and lifestyle of middle-class America.

But curiously enough, one of the most important underground comics, Gilbert Shelton's *Wonder Wart-Hog,*

216

first appeared in *Texas Ranger,* at the University of Texas. It then moved underground after its birth in a middle-class setting. It thus forms a neat parallel to the social movement of the readers of underground comics and even their creators.

There is a strange contradiction between the spirit of the underground comics and the heavy and rather pedantic kind of rationalizations and justifications which fans of these comics offer for their existence. In general the underground comics are spirited, uninhibited, zesty, and humorous. They joyfully revel in orgiastic sex and "put on" the straight people in society with very graphic and explicit evocations of every kind of sexual act conceivable—and some that are inconceivable. Other underground comics, however, are full of gore and horror—usually associated (also) with sexuality. Still others are simply satirical, and focus upon drugs and the hippie scene.

The names of the various underground comics are quite revealing, for they capture the ambience of the whole underground comics scene: *Grim Wit, Subvert Comics, Greaser (Stories to Dull the Imagination), The Fabulous Furry Freak Brothers, Motor City Comics, Big Ass Comics, Fritz the Cat, Mr. Natural, Despair Comics, Mother's Oats Comix, The New Adventures of Jesus, Amazon Comics, Feel Good Funnies, Up from the Deep, Rowlf, Fantagor, Skull, Slow Death, Hydrogen Bomb and Biochemical Warfare Funnies, Bijou, Fever Dreams, Turned On Cuties, Inner City Romance, Young Lust, Freakdope,* etc. The variety is astounding and the quality varies from rather pedestrian material to that which is worthy of serious attention. Some of these comics have nothing but shock value. Most of the artist themselves are terribly inconsistent—some of their work is good and some bad.

In the introduction to a collection of underground material, *The Best of the Rip Off Press Comix,* Volume One, there is a brief history of the underground movement which explains what underground comics try to do—blow people's minds with stories full of "lust, violence, pot, and politics." This thesis argues that ordinary middle-class people have become so inhibited and repressed by American society that it is necessary to take some rather extreme steps in order to reach them. This is the justification for underground comics—though most of their fans would also claim that the comics are intrinsically satisfying, that they are often very funny, have bizarre and freaky heroes and heroines, and are much more meaningful than the caped (and sexless) crusaders of yesteryear.

And yet, if society at large is repressive (and I'm not so certain that this is the case), I find these comics oppressive, as a rule, and curiously inhibited. They are, on the face of it, liberated and their characters revel in a compulsive and comic sexuality. There are frequent scenes of fellatio and cunnilingus, accompanied by large "slurps," to indicate the humor of it all.

But that is precisely the point. Sex is reduced to a kind of nonrelational and comic satisfaction of biological urges between people who seem to have no feelings about one another. "The extremes meet," it has been said—and the supersaturated sexuality of the underground comics leads, finally, to an almost Puritanical sense of sex as obligatory (as well as full of danger).

Marcuse has argued that the middle classes suffer from sexual desublimation—they sacrifice the pleasure of sensory or body experience to the reality principle. This desublimation, when institutionalized, leads to the development of the authoritarian personality and sets the stage for the development of fascism. But it seems to me that the characters in the underground comics suffer from a surfeit of sexual stimulation and do not have the benefit of either the reality principle or the pleasure principle.

The underground artists are so obsessed with outraging the middle classes that I cannot help but think they frequently cut off their noses (and at times, penises) to spite their faces. As such they reflect not a sense of liberation and freedom but of a rather narrow and forced libertinism. Their dissolute life style seems to be calculated and, really, not much fun.

The Rabelaisian ambience of freedom and ribaldry in the strips hides this neo-Puritanism quite effectively. The characters are generally bizarre—dope fiends, kooky gurus, mock superheroes, incredible animals, and so forth. And the adventures or stories, themselves, are frequently without endings, development, or anything structural. That is, much of the underground work is nonlinear and is not meant to tell a story. Rather, it seeks to create effects—frequently by means of fantastic art work. There is no question about the talent and imaginativeness of some of the underground artists—such as Schrier and Sheridan and

Moscoso—and they have done much to show the remarkable possibilities within the comic strip format.

Nevertheless I cannot help but sense an underlying joylessness and desperation. It may very well be that these artists (and their heroes) are linked too much to the very culture they are attempting to break away from. Revolutionaries are tied very strongly to that which they are revolting from—and even have a stake in the *status quo,* for without it, their revolutionary stance is impossible. Since successful revolutions inevitably lead to the triumph of bureaucrats and to repression, the counterculture comics artists are in a ticklish position. They find themselves in a love-hate relation to the culture in general, and all to frequently are more emotionally involved in what they are rejecting than they realize.

In fact, the direction people in a counter movement take is greatly determined by what they are attempting to escape. It also should be pointed out that underground comics are a media that feeds on the traditional media, much as one of the underground heroes, the Armadillo, feeds on heroes of the middle classes: soldiers, policemen, etc.

There are many parodies in the underground comics, and comic strip and comic book heroes are frequently ridiculed. But the underground comics also ridicule the absurdities of the counterculture as well as those of bourgeois culture. For example, one of the most interesting underground heroes is Robert Crumb's fake guru, Mr. Natural, a horny old man with a bald head and long flowing whiskers. His cohort is a seeker-after-knowledge named Flakey Foont, who never gains any satisfaction from Mr. Natural, and who is, in fact, frequently abused by him.

In one adventure, Mr. Natural is upset because his students haven't been paying him on time. He decides to change his image and goes to San Francisco, or as he puts it, "Ah! There's SHAM Francisco, where most of the deadbeats reside." He encounters Flakey Foont and tells him to drop out. Mr. Natural also reminds Flakey that he is $38.50 short on his payments. Foont then suggests, as a gag, that Mr. Natural drop out, which then prompts Mr. Natural to say:

YES! Of course! Why don't I? You'll get no more spiritual advice from dis holyman! As a guru I'm through. Goodbye.

Foont tries to go along, but Mr. Natural gives him a good kick in the pants, saying:

You go freeload off somebody else's psychic energy. G'wan! Beat it! Get stoned or something.

Mr. Natural goes to the Haight-Ashbury district where he encounters all kinds of people who want his advice. He runs into a hippie costume shop and emerges later in a disguise with sunglasses and a dark beard, only to find six other men, who look exactly like him and are stealing his stuff. The adventure ends with Mr. Natural splitting the scene and becoming Mr. "Snatcheral." The last panel shows him fornicating with a generously proportioned young lady who exclaims, as he pants and puffs, "Hey! Ya beard keeps ticklin' my nose!"

This little adventure certainly has a satirical dimension to it; it suggests that there is a great deal that is fraudulent and even silly in mysticism. After all, Mr. Natural is a fake and his disciple Flakey is a fool: so much of a fool, in fact, that he thinks his *guru* has great powers and refuses to be disillusioned. It is obvious that Mr. Natural has a good thing for himself and is more concerned about being paid for his services than anything else—except, perhaps, the chance to ride in Flakey's car and fornicate.

In fact, Mr. Natural seems to have contempt for Flakey and all that he stands for. (Mr. Natural frequently tries to get rid of Flakey by suggesting he take dope and get stoned!) Mr. Natural is really a conservative character who is playing the guru for all it is worth; he dupes the well-intentioned but naive members of the counterculture, who lack discrimination, but seem to have discretionary income. He is the perfect prototype of the *hip capitalist* and seems to have nothing but contempt for those who follow him and are exploited by him.

This element in Mr. Natural is in keeping with Crumb's essentially conservative beliefs. In a proclamation, entitled "And Now a Word to You Feminist Women," Crumb castigates the women's liberation movement and women who have suggested that his work is sexist. He concludes his statement with the following:

> Well, listen, you dumb-assed broads, I'm gonna draw what I fucking-well please to draw, and if you don't like it, FUCK YOU!

He argues that as an artist he should be free to draw whatever he wants; otherwise he could become a propagandist for movements and his artistic integrity would be compromised.

There is a good deal to be said for this argument, though I don't happen to agree with Crumb—because art is implicitly social and political, no matter what the artist thinks he is doing or not doing. But the important thing to notice is that Crumb has been attacked for the rather savage way women are treated in his comics. As he puts it:

> I don't deny that my cartoons contain a great deal of hostile and often brutal acts against women! I'm well aware of this dark side of my ego!

He pleads, then, that though he portrays brutal things, he does not advocate such things by any means.

Whether he does or doesn't is not the issue; what is important here is that the underground comics reflect attitudes that are not healthy, though the basic stance of these comics is that they are free and represent liberated minds, which have escaped from the oppressive nature of bourgeois society. The underground artists have reacted against the mushy absurdities of romantic love and all the commercialism and nonsense that is connected with it. But they have moved too far in the opposite direction and have not been content to take the idealized female off her pedestal. They have, all too often, insisted on shoving her into the gutter and debasing her.

I might point out that there are some artists who are relatively sympathetic to women. In a *Trashman* adventure entitled "Trashman Meets the Fighting She Devils," the plot is based on a reversal of "the whole sexual dominance relationship traditional to our civilization." We find women as the dominant element—fighting, and killing, and sexually predatory, in an ironic reversal of roles, meant to demonstrate, graphically, the inequities and evils in our society.

Trashman and his companion Dr. Eugene Cranker are riding down a highway when they innocently intrude in a battle between an army of men and their attackers. The army is wiped out, and Trashman and his companion are captured—by a horde of warlike women who abuse them violently. Trashman and Cranker are taken to the women's camp where they are gangbanged.

The intent of the story is to show how women are abused and exploited by men though, curiously enough, this is done in a story which, like the others I have described, shows women as destructive killers.

A famous church father once said that woman is "a temple over a sewer." The underground comics have, I'm afraid, focused too much on women as a sewer, and in their zeal to demythologize and deromanticize women, have dehumanized her.

Perhaps Mr. Natural and Trashman are symbolic heroes who represent, in vague ways, infantile disorders of the cerebellum and the crotch. Both are comic figures, both parody heroic types (the guru and the superhero), and both tell us a great deal more than they think about both the counterculture and our so-called straight culture. The underground comics show that the comic strip/book format is a medium with enormous versatility; indeed, the comic book has become one of the most important media of satire and social criticism in the 1970s, though it remains quite infantile. Whether the independent comic book artist with a vision will flourish and develop, or whether this form of artistry will be captured by hip capitalists (with beards and dark glasses, like Mr. Natural and the various fake Mr. Naturals), remains to be seen.